Barclay & Crousse

Landscapes of Intimacy

Barclay & Crousse
Landscapes of Intimacy

First edition, 2020
ISBN 978-607-9489-72-4

MCHAP
This publication and the Mies Crown Hall Americas Prize (MCHAP) are initiatives of Illinois Institute of Technology's College of Architecture.

MCHAP would like to thank all those who made this program and publication possible: IIT, the College of Architecture and the Lambert Fund, the City of Chicago, and the firms, institutions, and individuals that generously support the initiative, including the Canadian Centre for Architecture, The Alphawood Foundation, Kohler, and the Mies van der Rohe Society at Illinois Institute of Technology.

Illinois Institute of Technology
Reed Kroloff, Dean of Illinois Institute of Technology's College of Architecture
Dirk Denison, MCHAP Director
Sasha Zanko, MCHAP Coordinator

Published by:

© IITAC Press
College of Architecture
3360 South State Street
Chicago, IL
60616-3793,
USA
arch.iit.edu

© Arquine, S.A. de C.V.
Ámsterdam 163 A
Colonia Hipódromo, 06100
Mexico City
arquine.com

Texts by:
© Miquel Adrià
© Sandra Barclay
© Jean Pierre Crousse
© Dirk Denison
© Mario Vargas Llosa

Images by:
© Cristóbal Palma, except:
© Barclay & Crousse Office: p. 42 (figs. 02, 04, 09 and 10), p. 70 (figs. 02-07), p. 98 (figs. 04 and 06), p. 132 (figs. 08 and 09)
© Eugène Courret: p. 132 (fig. 02)
© Jaime Rouillon + Barclay & Crousse Office: p. 132 (fig. 06)
© Jean Pierre Crousse: p. 42 (figs. 03, 06 and 07), p. 70 (fig. 01), p. 98 (figs. 01-03, 05, 07 and 08), p. 128 (figs. 01-04), p. 132 (figs. 05-09), p. 160 (figs. 01, 03-05 and 07)
© Richard Long: p. 42 (fig. 01)
© Servicio Aerofotográfico Nacional: p. 42 (figs. 05 and 08)

Director
Miquel Adrià

Editorial Director
Brenda Soto

Editorial Assistance
Valeria Fuentes

Design
Ápice | Diego Beauroyre, Maira Fragoso and Rebeca Mora

Translation and Copy Editing
Fionn Petch
Quentin Pope

Prepress
A. Andrés Monroy

Barclay & Crousse

Landscapes of Intimacy

Photography by Cristóbal Palma

Preface

Dirk Denison

The College of Architecture at Illinois Institute of Technology (IIT) established the Mies Crown Hall Americas Prize (MCHAP) in 2012 to recognize architectural excellence in the Americas. MCHAP seeks out contemporary projects that speak to architecture's fundamental power to shape communities for the better. By drawing sustained attention to works that set new precedents for life in our complex and dynamic world, the prize celebrates the potential of our art.

In 2018, the MCHAP jury selected Barclay & Crousse's Edificio E, a building on the campus of the University of Piura, in Peru, as the winner of the Americas Prize. The Americas Prize, MCHAP's main award, honors an exceptional work of architecture realized in the Americas in the previous two years. (The companion Prize for Emerging Practice recognizes a work from the same time frame by a practice in its first ten years of operation.) That MCHAP is housed in a university is central to our project; its mandate is not only to uncover what architectural excellence looks like, but to absorb and share its lessons—with students, the profession, and leaders and citizens. MCHAP winners visit IIT to lecture and work with students and faculty; the prize also supports the development of publications, including this one, that disseminate these lessons even further.

This book presents the thinking that has informed Barclay & Crousse's decades-long practice. First bi-continentally and now primarily in their home country of Peru, Sandra Barclay and Jean Pierre Crousse have undertaken a continual and extraordinarily sensitive exploration of how architecture relates to contemporary conditions. Their work is both modest and striking; it foregrounds human interactions and connections, particularly a connection to location—to a project's natural, material, and social contexts. As a testament to the relevance of their approach, three additional Barclay & Crousse projects have been nominated for the Americas Prize: Equis House, a home organized around a courtyard protecting residents from the desert, completed in 2003 at La Escondida Beach, Peru; the Place of Remembrance, built on the cliffs of Lima in 2010; and the Paracas Museum, also in Peru, a cultural site rebuilt after an earthquake, finished in 2016.

The MCHAP process taps into a global network of nominators, which includes not only architects but representatives of fields as diverse as policymaking and cooking. Around two hundred projects have been nominated in each of the three MCHAP cycles, creating a powerful catalog of contemporary architecture, vetted by those with direct experience of the works and the meaningful impact they've had on their inhabitants and communities. The Place of Remembrance, in particular, stands out in this sense: it is a site that confronts Peruvians with the violence of the country's recent past (specifically, the terrorism of the Shining Path in the 1980s) within a dramatic natural context that evokes a much broader history. We are remarkably privileged to have the legendary writer and Nobel Prize-winner Mario Vargas Llosa, who initiated that project, as a contributor to this volume.

Edificio E was among six works named as finalists for the 2018 Americas Prize—all distinguished projects that testify to the current strength and inventiveness of architecture in the Americas. The 2018 jury was led by Ricky Burdett, CBE, and included Mexico City-based architect Jose Castillo, IIT faculty member and landscape architect Ron Henderson, architect Rodrigo Pérez de Arce from Santiago, Chile, and architect Claire Weisz from New York City. Burdett characterized the works the jury was drawn to as explorations of "the spatial potential of economy of means with maximum impact...We were not looking for architectural pyrotechnics," Burdett explained at the finalist announcement event. "We were interested in buildings that work—for the city, for the institution, for the neighborhood, community, and the individual occupants."

Set in a dry forest in northern Peru, Edificio E is an accomplished example of exactly this: converting a simple concept into a meaningful communal experience, what Barclay & Crousse have called a "learning landscape." The building provides a new centerpiece for a dispersed campus, offering students a place to meet or just rest in the shade. It carves complex but informal spaces out of a geometric mass inserted into, but still in tune with, its desert context. (Weisz remarked that Edificio E was "perhaps the first building I have seen where the trees were as important as the classrooms.") Just as Mies van der Rohe's S. R. Crown Hall, another educational building and MCHAP's home base, brought forward new understandings of how architecture defines and encloses space, Edificio E activates the spaces between to enhance qualities of interaction, extending our collective architectural language.

The project is also the result of the steadfast commitment and vision of the University of Piura and its research vice provost, Maria Pia Chirinos, who partnered with the architects in creating a transformative building for their campus. This particular relationship and the unique collaborative process it allowed is one of several topics Barclay & Crousse have addressed in conversation with Reed Kroloff, the dean of the IIT College of Architecture—discussions that took place as an extension of their residency in Crown Hall in the spring of 2020, and which are highlighted in the introduction to the project later in this book.

During their visit to Chicago, Barclay & Crousse also interacted with students and faculty in critiques and workshops, and shared their ideas with the public in a city with a specific connection to architecture and its recent history. This direct engagement, this exchange of perspectives, is at the core of MCHAP. Since 2012, I have seen firsthand how the relationships MCHAP has forged can bridge what seems like an impossible diversity: two continents of one billion people, 80 percent of whom live in distinct, and distinctly vibrant, urban configurations. We are grateful to have Barclay & Crousse as our partners, whose particular practice—embedded in Peru, but oriented toward a wider humanity—shows us what an architecture of place can mean on a global scale.

Barclay & Crousse: Networks and Places

Barclay & Crousse stand out in the landscape of Latin American architecture. Perhaps due to Peru's challenging political situation, Sandra Barclay (Lima, 1967) and Jean Pierre Crousse (Lima, 1963) pursued an unusual career path that led them to complete their academic and professional training in Paris. They produced their first projects for Peru while still based in France, before eventually returning to their country of origin. Yet this distance afforded them a perspective to identify themselves as more fully Peruvian; while working from afar on their first three houses, they reflected on their home country's exceptional conditions. After spending 16 years in Paris, they have lived and worked in Lima since 2006, where they have built a number of projects for private clients (beach houses, city apartments, restaurants, and more), as well as taking public commissions enabling them to propose some bold ideas that go beyond the architectural program. As a result, their architecture has not only been covered by specialist media; it has had a broader, cross-cutting impact on the national psyche. In this sense the Place of Remembrance is not merely the result of a program or a professional stubbornness to swim against the current, but instead shapes a new urban landscape that understands and completes Lima's boundaries. No less important is the studio's project for the University of Piura's new lecture halls and faculty offices. This building is a departure from the layout of the original campus, serving a range of functions as a self-contained city inserted in the middle of northern Peru's desert landscape. However, Barclay & Crousse do not just create architecture based on powerful concepts; their constructions are superbly crafted and reveal a well-trained eye for composition and proportions. They are also skilled in the use of light, color and materials for flat surfaces, and their structures are executed with scientific precision.

Working in Peru requires engaging in a constant dialogue with memory and the territory. Complexity is inherent in a country whose ancient pre-Hispanic culture is blended with a colonial legacy, overlaid with modernity and a developing economy. William Curtis wrote that "Latin American identity should be carefully analyzed for what it is: an ideological weave that has wrestled with integrating the new and the old, Hispanic and pre-Hispanic traditions, center and religion, city and countryside, cosmopolitan and indigenous worlds, modernity and *mestizaje*, domestic and international influences."[1] Latin American culture has evolved in this way throughout the 20th century, alternating between uncritical, internationalist modernity and the championing of local architecture, produced with a limited range of vernacular materials and eschewing the latest technologies. There has been a tendency to over-generalize by boiling down certain attributes to original, national conditions: in Mexico architecture is monumental, in Colombia it's all about material qualities, in Brazil it focuses on structural formalism, in Chile it dwells on the landscape, and so on. When visiting Barclay & Crousse's buildings, where the surrounding territory provides a constant reference point, we need to ask what makes it unique, or what reveals its Peruvian origin. This

Miquel Adrià

1 William Curtis, "Lo general y lo local. Casa del arquitecto Enrique del Moral en la calle Francisco Ramírez, 5, Ciudad de México, 1948", in *Modernidad y arquitectura en México*, Edward Burian (ed.), Barcelona: Gustavo Gili, 1997, p. 120.

shows us that their architecture does not stand out for its monumentality or its connection to the landscape; it is a landscape in itself. This quality is evident in their beach houses at La Escondida Beach, and particularly in the Place of Remembrance. Their work also explores the potential of matter, the depth of their façades blurring the boundaries between interior and exterior space, and holding sacred some of their shared public spaces, as in the Piura university building, for example, where the extraordinary forms part of everyday life.

For Iñaki Ábalos, the consolidation of "modernist Latin American architecture had a heroic and identity-based dimension well into the 1980s, following four principal vectors: Latin America's territorial specificities and its pre-Columbian heritage; its present, with its cultural ties to Europe and the Americas; vernacular techniques and a specific natural and climactic environment; and a social milieu that aspired to become more visible to the outside world. What is interesting," continues Ábalos, "in now seeing the architecture produced in the last decade in cities like Medellín, Santiago, Lima, Buenos Aires, Montevideo, Mexico City, and so many others in Latin America, is not only that these vectors have decisively contributed to the creation of magnificent architecture, but also that today they are all appearing on the same playing field... It is at once multifaceted and universal, complex and simple, capable of producing works and projects that are interesting as genuine expressions of what architecture can produce in contemporary culture."[2]

In line with Ábalos's upbeat reading, as Peru has flourished economically in recent decades several architecture and a number of two-member architectural teams have formed: Ruth Alvarado and Óscar Borasino, Patricia Llosa and Rodolfo Cortegana, Alfredo Benavides and Cynthia Watmough, and Jean Pierre Crousse and Sandra Barclay, who have developed a refined and self-contained approach, echoing contemporary trends and the prevailing ideas in the European and US schools where they trained.[3] Whereas some of these duos (such as Alvarado and Borasino) achieve a serene modernity to match their place of origin and era,[4] and others (for example Llosa and Cortegana) dive deeper into the variations in domestic typologies in connection to program, context and construction systems,[5] Barclay & Crousse start out with the concept to be developed before tackling the space itself. Alejandro de la Sota proposed keeping a distance from outward appearances and underscored the central importance of the idea: "...like an initiation ritual, it becomes necessary to get rid of accessories and phenomenological elements in order to drill down to the essence, the idea."[6] In common with this remarkable 20th-cen-

2 Iñaki Ábalos, "Latin American Architecture Today," Harvard Design Magazine 34, 2011. Cited in my text for the book *Radical: 50 arquitecturas de América Latina*, Mexico City: Arquine, 2016, p. 9.

3 Miquel Adrià, "Arquitecturas entrecruzadas," in *OB+RA*, Mexico City: Arquine, 2016, p. 209.

4 *Idem.*

5 Miquel Adrià, "Llosa Cortegana: la arquitectura está en la sección," in *La casa es una idea*, Mexico City: Arquine, 2019, p. 9.

6 Josep Lluís Mateo, "Sentiment i raó," *Quaderns d'Arquitectura i Urbanismo* 152, 1982, p. 9.

tury Spanish architect, Barclay & Crousse have a passion for what is essential, the strictly necessary, and their work is increasingly stripped down as they became more rooted in the Peruvian context, letting go of the more fanciful French influence of their early years. They share De la Sota's fascination with extended volumes, which they excavate to create continuous planar movements that qualify and define space, in the tradition of Guiseppe Terragni's façades, notable in De la Sota's city council building in Tarragona and in Barclay & Crousse's M6 House, where the planes converge along their edges in a virtual manner. Displaying a kinship with the late-modern language of the Five Architects or the post-Corbusianism of Henri Ciriani, with whom Jean Pierre worked in his Paris office, some projects inherit compositional axes not only in their façades' planes but also in defining the volume enclosed by them, such as in the interior volume of Murisis House. Their beach houses, meanwhile, use topographical sections to blend into the desert landscape of the Pacific coastline, inserting concrete sheets perpendicular to the coast as perimeter walls with openings to ventilate and illuminate the interiors. The Kahnian notion of "served" and "servant" spaces is another constant in many of their works, in which the thickness of the walls (in the Museum of Paracas, or the UN Park Apartments, for example) are used to house servant and circulation spaces. Given the opportunity for working in a country with an extremely mild climate and where it never rains, they use the ambiguity between interior and exterior in the ambivalence of the spaces, the architectural route through them, and cross-ventilation. It is no coincidence that, upon graduating, Jean Pierre Crousse worked as an assistant lecturer in Environmental Studies.

After many trials and tribulations (competition entries, buildings, political troubles, and so on) Barclay & Crousse incorporated the landscape as an iconic feature based on the Corbusian fretted section in the Paracas Museum, and subsequently at the University of Piura they put into practice their well-honed intuitions. The new university building that houses lecture halls for teaching a range of subjects is a small urban center in the middle of the semi-desert landscape, and has apertures both on its vertical planes that are otherwise almost blind, as well as in its roof. One section that interprets an imaginary forest creates a first floor of tree trunks and a second floor of canopies, allowing sunlight to filter through, marking the time of day on the floor in one direction, and the seasons of the year in the other. The expressive power of the structures and painted communal spaces, along with the corridors and ramps crossing the interior pathways, are another example of Corbusian influence. A legacy that subtly emerges once again in the skylights of the building's façades opposite the United Nations park in Lima, and in the structural prisms of their house in Huayoccari, mirroring the outline of the mountains to frame the best views of the spectacular surroundings.

Yet Barclay & Crousse's work is not just the result of territorial legacies; it is a complex interweaving of connections mutually enriched by other cultures and locations. Sandra and Jean Pierre are part of a generation that includes Angelo Bucci from São Paulo, Mauricio Rocha from Mexico City, Solano Benítez from Asunción, Sebastián Irarrázaval and Smiljan Radic from Santiago de Chile, Daniel Bonilla

from Bogotá, Mónica Bertolino and Carlos Barrado from Córdoba, and of course Fernando Viegas and Alvaro Puntoni, also from São Paulo. In fact their relation began on their return from Paris, and it was in Lima where they began to develop shared interests, while they maintained their connection to Laurent and Emmanuelle Beaudouin, a former partner for various projects with their collaborators and partners from Atelier Nord Sud, and with the UNO group directed by their mentor, Ciriani, in Paris-Belleville. Curiously, the connection with Chicago's IIT—which awarded them the prestigious Mies Crown Hall Americas Prize in 2018—developed later, after a period of academic involvement at GSD, with Felipe Correa and Rahul Mehrotra.

This professional and personal relationship helps contextualize the work of Sandra Barclay and Jean Pierre Crousse, not only in the Peruvian milieu but across an entire continent where they work today, in their practice (that began in Paris and continued in Lima) and in their teaching work at Harvard's Graduate School of Design (GSD), Yale and at the PUCP (Pontificia Universidad Católica de Perú). There is no doubt that Barclay & Crousse are among the brightest stars in the Latin American architectural universe today.

I

The Space of Tolerance

The Place of Remembrance

The Place of Remembrance, Tolerance and Social Inclusion was the subject of an intense national debate in 2010. I became involved in the discussion, writing articles and giving interviews in support of the idea that Peruvians should have the opportunity to reflect and seek reconciliation following the terrible conflict of the 1980s. With its epicenter in the Ayacucho department, the violence left in its wake a horrific legacy of 60,000 dead, tens of thousands wounded, and unprecedented destruction in central Peru's Andean region. As a result of this debate, President Alan García Pérez invited a group of people who had defended this proposal to meet in the home of the distinguished anthropologist Juan Ossio Acuña, and suggested we form a commission, which I was to preside. The outcome has been this institution that fortunately has existed for several years as testimony to the events of that tragic period, and which further serves as a point of contact for the museums and places of memory that have emerged across the whole country.

To build the Place of Remembrance, we launched a national competition with a jury comprising Kenneth Frampton, Rafael Moneo and Francesco Dal Co, along with the Peruvians Wiley Ludeña and José García Bryce. The project received generous donations from the governments of Germany, Sweden, and the European Union, and it was implemented by United Nations Development Programme (UNDP). The architects behind the winning scheme, Sandra Barclay and Jean Pierre Crousse, won the prestigious Oscar Niemeyer prize for the best new building in Latin America.

Since its inauguration, and amidst constant controversy, the Place of Remembrance is today a solid reality and is widely seen to be a highly valuable institution as a museum of history and a center of research. It has already had a number of directors, and varying levels of support from successive governments. Its exhibitions have objectively presented the many contributing factors to the lamentable events that embroiled so many Peruvians, the vast majority from peasant farmer families, in the cruelties of an ideological war, and the conflict's effect on society at large. Despite the many criticisms about the Place of Remembrance—some with a very self-interested agenda—my impression is that those who visit and understand its research and educational purpose find it true to its founding intentions. These objectives lay an important foundation—though one that can always be perfected—for avoiding the recurrence of a war of this kind in our country. Its aim of reconciliation is being fulfilled.

For those of us who sat on the first of many commissions responsible for the Place of Remembrance, this institution was not intended to be solely academic. Rather, it should be a stout defender of democracy and peace, rejecting all ideologies that justify resorting to violence as a tool of political action. In other words, it should resolutely uphold freedom and the rule of law, elected governments in transparent and democratic elections, which guarantee freedom of expression and the right to criticize, and resolve all conflicts through informed debate and constitutional rights.

The site chosen for this beautiful and functional building designed by Sandra Barclay and Jean Pierre Crousse is exceptional. Perched on the clifftops from which Lima contemplates the Pacific

Mario Vargas Llosa

Ocean, it is perhaps the city's most beautiful spectacle, and its spacious galleries create room for exhibitions of all kinds, on social and political aspects of the present day and recent past, while offering scholars a peaceful and stimulating space for research and reflection. On my last visit to Lima, I found it very stimulating to meet the students of all backgrounds who were working in the museum, as well as to converse with the current director, historian Juan Manuel Burga. We spoke of my alma mater, the University of San Marcos, where he had been an eminent provost.

Certainly, many things still need to be fine-tuned for the Place of Remembrance to achieve its full potential. But its mere existence is already a magnificent achievement. It signifies choosing civilized debate instead of an adversary's extermination and bloodletting; peaceful coexistence in diversity instead of ideological war; votes instead of bullets; and democratic values instead of bloodthirsty actions. The Place of Remembrance is also the symbol of a history that must never be repeated in Peru.

Madrid, December 2019

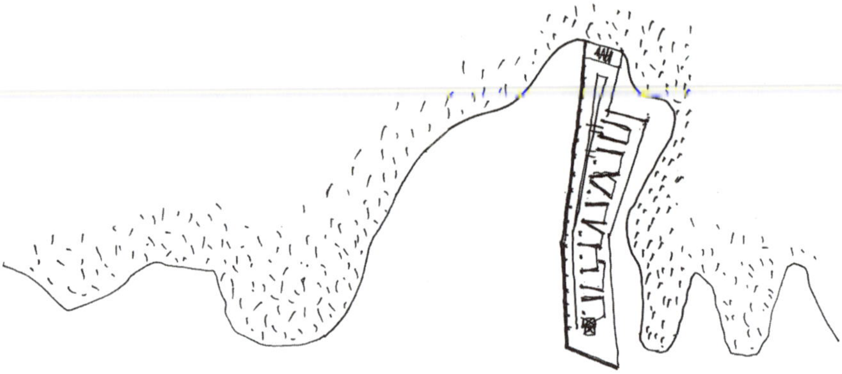

Place of Remembrance

Location
Miraflores, Lima, Peru

Schedule
CONTEST March 2010
PROJECT May — November 2010
WORK June 2011 — March 2014
MUSEOGRAPHY October — December 2015

Lot Area
7,573 m²

Floor Area
4,896 m²

Client
High-Commission for the Management and Implementation of the Museum of Remembrance / United Nations Development Programme (UNDP)

Design Team
CONTEST CONSULTANCY
Roberto Huarcaya fotógrafo
CONTEST Eduardo Zambrano, Sebastián Cillóniz, Alessandra Calmell, Carlos Fernandez, Rosa Aguirre
PROJECT MANAGER Paulo Shimabukuro
OUTDOOR SPACES CONSULTANCY
Verónica Crousse escultora
WORK SUPERVISION Mauricio Sialer

Structural Engineering
Raúl Ríos

Sanitary Installation
Roberto Paín

Electrical Installation
Walter Palomino

Construction
ALTESA

Funding
German Agency for International Cooperation (GIZ) / Swedish Government, European Union / Government of Peru

Launched in 2010 by a high-level commission led by Peruvian writer and Nobel laureate Mario Vargas Llosa, the Place of Remembrance, Tolerance and Social Inclusion, or LUM, was created as a place of reconciliation for Peruvians after two decades of deadly violence during which more than 70,000 people were killed. The LUM is designed not only to inform visitors about this extremely bloody conflict, but also to connect the many different museums and sites preserving the memory of this conflict across the country that have been created by victim associations, without official support.

A national competition was held to choose the winning project, with international jury members Kenneth Frampton, Rafael Moneo and Francesco dal Co working alongside Peruvians Wiley Ludeña and José García Bryce. Funding came from the German and Swedish governments, the European Union, and the construction itself was managed by the United Nations development program (UNDP).

The Place of Remembrance is embedded in the cliff-edge that defines Lima's bay, blending into this area of outcrops and ravines. The design "stitches together" the wound caused by the construction of a road leading down from the city to the beaches at the foot of the cliffs. Forming a type of "artificial outcrop", the compact construction is nestled into a landscape eroded by natural forces, almost as a geographical extension of a topological system stretching more than 10 kilometers from the far south of the bay to the site of the project.

To add a temporal and spatial dimension to this project, we saw potential in the long and narrow access route from the public highway to the lot. This prepares visitors and provides them a meaningful experience by dislocating them from their everyday lives. The route begins on the public highway, continues down a fault or ravine cleaved between the building and the natural outcrop, emulating the typical way down to beach on the bay. The experience is articulated by an experiential journey through the collection and ends with the walk back toward the city, through a series of open-air and roofed spaces that predispose visitors to interact with the museum exhibits.

The ground is terraced, providing independent access to other parts of the program such as the research center and the auditorium. These terraces create a large public space for the city, despite not being a requirement in the competition brief. The same material as found in the cliffs is used for the paving and the building—cobblestones, gravel and sand. The area is also marked by the plants that grow naturally on this and other ravines in the bay. This shared space expresses the building's institutionality and public status.

The design's proper orientation and careful placement of apertures and choice of materials enhances the acoustic and visual comfort. This prevents direct solar gain and avoids the need for air conditioning, reducing the energy footprint as efficiently as possible. The fire-fighting water storage tank is positioned along the edge of the public esplanade, creating a transitional space between this area and the ocean. Gray waters are treated for irrigation of adjacent green areas, meaning the building does not need to be connected to the sewer mains, which is located higher up the slope, thus saving the energy cost of pumping.

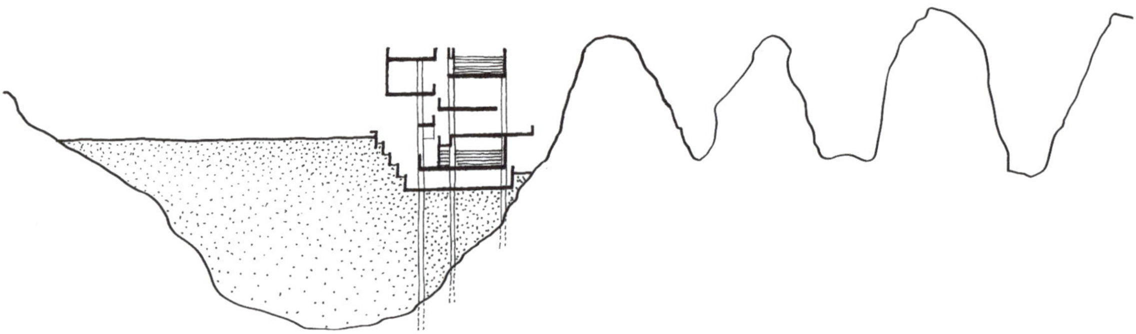

0 30

A-A Section B-B Section

Level 1 and 2 floor plans Access and -1 level (auditorium) floor plans

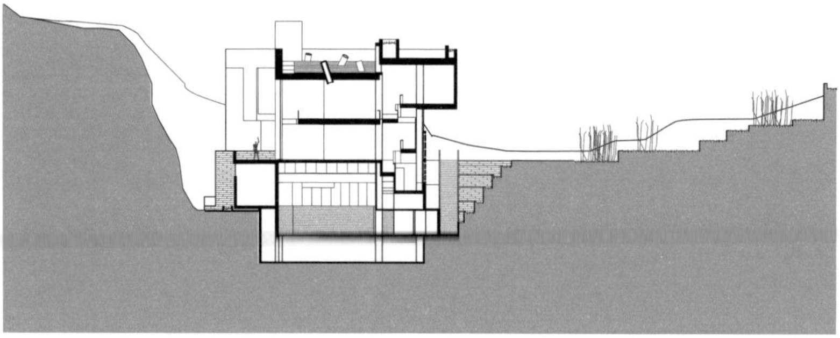

0 50

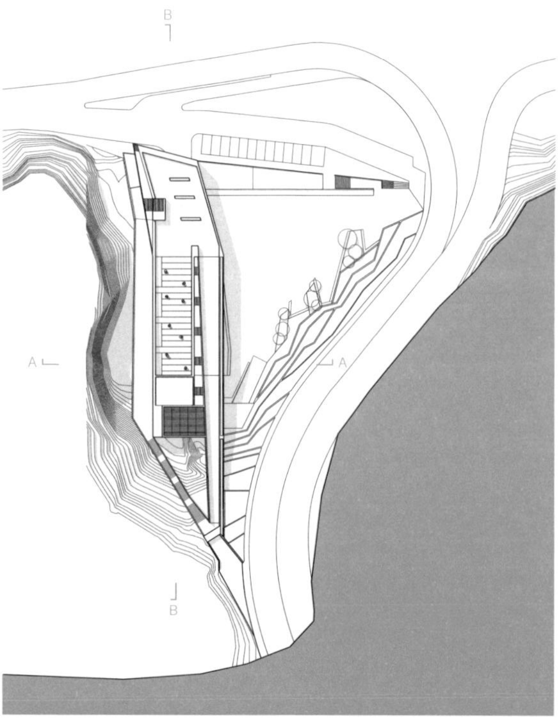

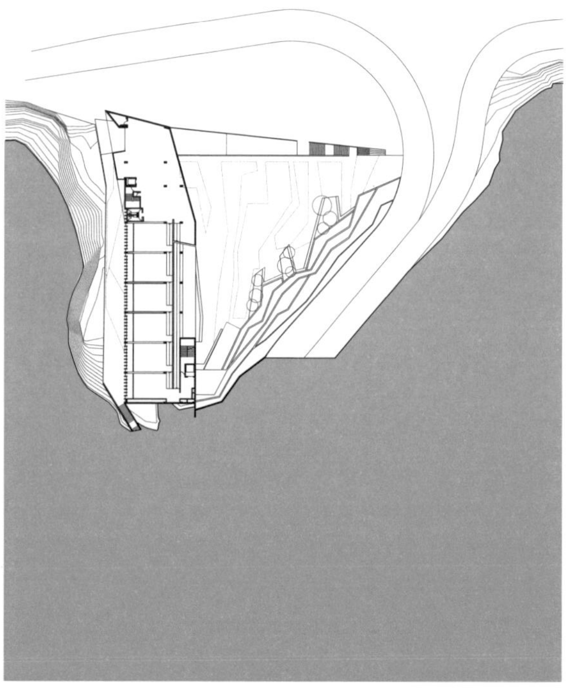

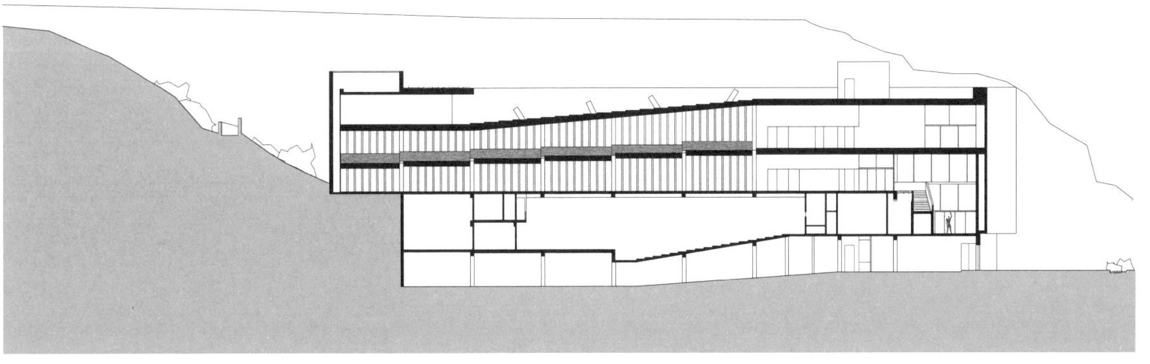

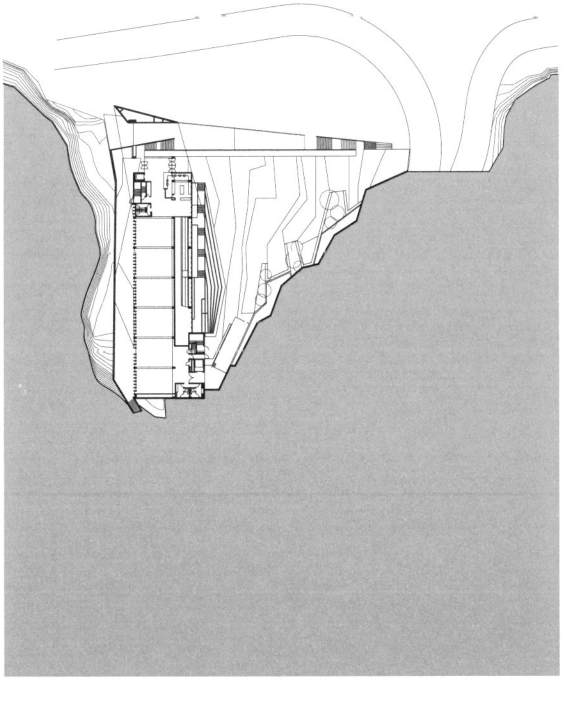

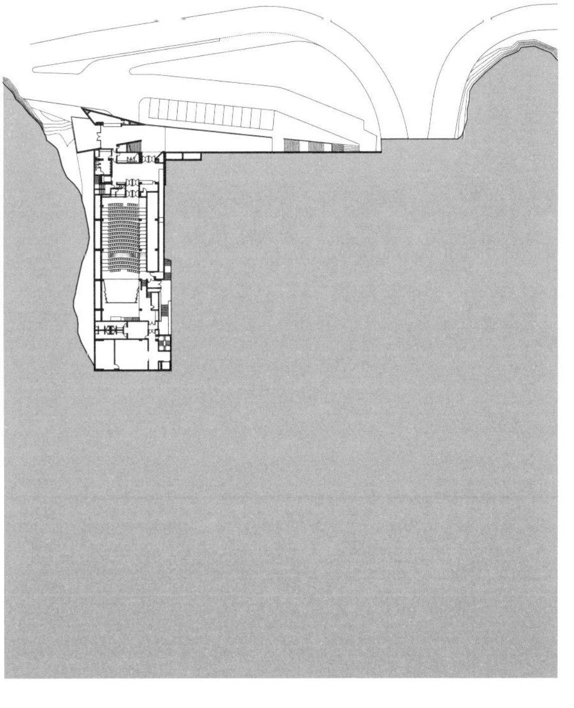

DAÑOS MATERIALES
Y ECONÓMICOS

NI CON BALAS

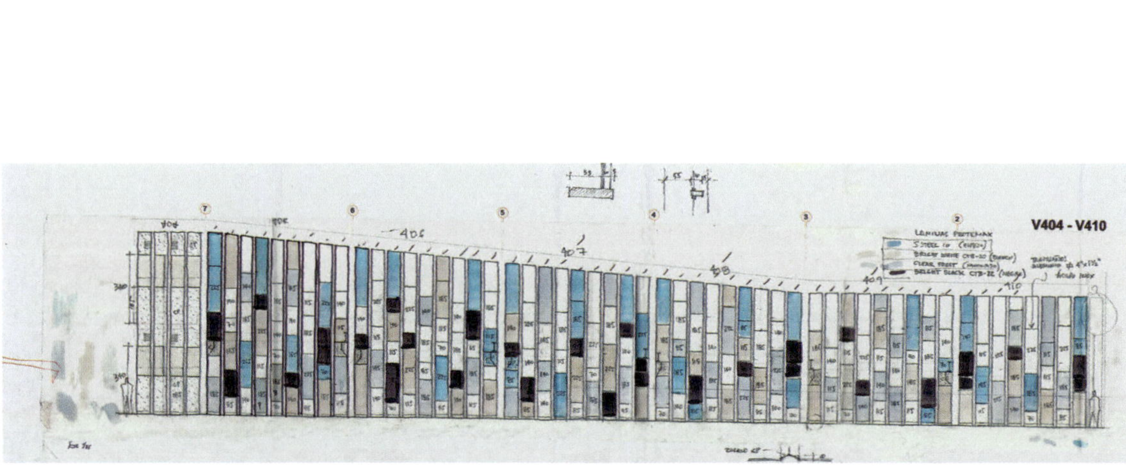
V404 - V410

Ayqispa yacharaniku

II

The Patient Search

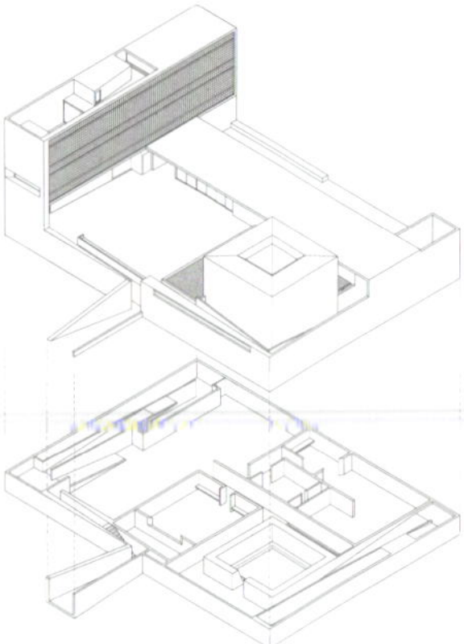

Fig. 10. Turrell Museum, axonometric

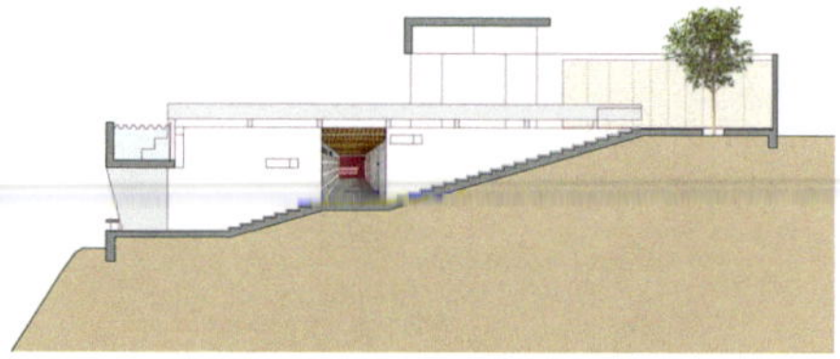

Figs. 03 and 04. Equis House, pool and longitudinal section

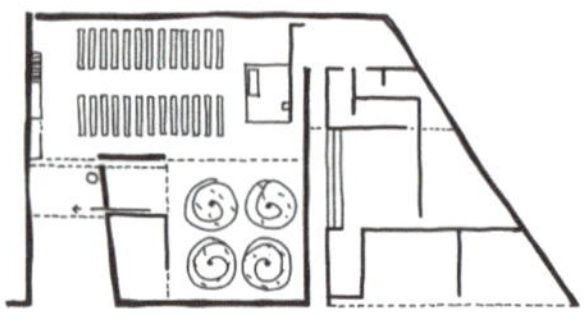

Fig. 09. Santa Cruz de Asia Church, plan

Fig. 05. Pachacamac, 1943

Fig. 08. Puruchuco before its restoration

Fig. 02. Turrell Museum and Equis House, photomontage

Fig. 06. Vedoble Houses

Fig. 07. Equis House

Fig. 01. Walking a Line in Peru

Landscapes and Microcosms

Sandra Barclay
Jean Pierre Crousse

As young graduates, circumstances took us to Europe to continue our education as architects. Some years later, in 1994, we set up our own studio in Paris. The sixteen years we spent in such an unfamiliar milieu taught us the importance of having grown up on the arid desert coast of Peru, a region with a unique climate, inhabited continuously for thousands of years; traces of past civilizations are still visible even in our home city of Lima. After 1998, having completed a number of projects in France, we were given the opportunity—while still based in Paris—to design a series of summer houses on the Peruvian coast.

The distance in both geography and in climate was decisive in clarifying what we wanted to explore: we took the commission as a pretext to rethink the connections that architecture can forge, not only with our home region's unique landscape, culture, and climate, but also to take a fresh approach to its underlying concepts. The Peruvian coast—which enjoys a mild climate without a marked difference between day and night-time temperatures or between summer and winter, lacks precipitation, storms or strong winds, and is even spared harsh tropical sunlight due to the prevailing mist—seems to defy the very idea of architecture having to offer shelter.

The lineage that goes from the cave to Marc-Antoine Laugier's hut loses relevance in such a context. The house is relieved of the requirement to provide shelter and only needs to offer the necessary privacy for living within the vast expanse of desert. Domestic architecture no longer refers to the refuge offered by the cave and instead naturally aspires to a cosmic connection, as in the case of sacred buildings such as the Stonehenge trilithon and pre-Hispanic architecture's platforms and enclosures. Designs can concentrate on establishing an intelligible order of the cosmos, infused with a meaning more closely connected to human aspirations and their relationship with the world than to offering shelter from natural hazards. As explained by Christian Norberg-Schulz, dwelling is conditioned by the construction of a sensitive and significant connection between human beings and their surroundings, a process that needs understanding and identification.[1]

Equis House, the third project in the series of houses designed for La Escondida Beach at our Paris studio, was vital in showing us our responsibility when faced with design possibilities. We understood that producing meaningful architecture in this setting meant relinquishing our desire to connect to the landscape with a clearly identifiable architectural object inserted within it. Our ambition was to create spaces capable of revealing the place, so that the architecture could be just as dependent on the landscape, understood in the broadest sense of the term, as the other way around. The intervention had to reveal some qualities of the site while hiding others, with the emergence of the new reality that we were building. We consider that architecture is faced with the challenge of acquiring a new meaning for itself in relation to the landscape, in the same way that the landscape acquires a new significance due to the architectural artifact.

Abandoning the idea of subjugating the landscape with a sublime object that relates to its surroundings due to its singularity and

1 Christian Norberg-Schulz, *L'Abitare (The Concept of Dwelling)*, Milan: Electa, 1984, p. 13.

autonomy is something that can be clearly seen in Richard Long's work. With "Walking a Line in Peru," his intervention creates "one more layer, a mark, laid upon the thousands of other layers of human and geographic history on the surface of the land".[2] (*Fig. 01*)

In Equis House, creating a microcosm as a means of living in intimacy within the surrounding vastness was a learning process that transformed an intuition into an active search some years later with the (unbuilt) project for the Turrell Museum, next door to the house. (*Fig. 02*)

While Gaston Bachelard considered the house a world in itself, a world of human experience,[3] we think that the house must also be capable of condensing and appropriating its surroundings to give inhabitants a sense of belonging to the place. Alexander von Humboldt, whom we admire for having understood that the Central Andes are only comprehensible in section, used the term "cosmos" to express and encapsulate the sky and the earth as a single entity.[4]

In the same way, we wanted Equis House to embody—on an architectural scale—the section of the coast running from the Pacific Ocean and the desert to the fertile Andean valleys. The longitudinal section frames the sky, emerging from the suspended swimming pool (which brings the immensity of the ocean into the foreground), following the slope of the stairs, and ending with a tree protected by an enclosure at the upper level. (*Figs. 03 and 04*)

If the section reveals the territory, the volumetric and formal expression seeks to blend into the desert's vastness with an equivalent level of abstraction. In this case, the architectural abstraction owes nothing to European pictorial tradition, as happened with modern architecture, but instead responds to the desire to alter the scale. The desert—which lacks measurable or identifiable features such as vegetation due to its size—blurs the boundaries between shape and background, and turns the landscape into a single element that fades into the distance and accentuates its abstraction. Seen from a contemporary standpoint, many remains of the past seem to follow this approach by appearing on the landscape as abstract volumes, either extruded or excavated. (*Fig. 05*)

For Equis House, we removed architectural features such as doors, handrails and windows that give the complex its scale, but without it losing human aspect. The house's interior is carefully arranged: the human body is used as the reference for the space's dimensions. The scale is given by the occupants themselves, their furniture and their objects. In his phenomenological study of inhabitation, Norberg-Schulz highlights how the identification we need to dwell in a place is mediated by our significant relation with things.[5] The house as a microcosm of territory becomes one of those things and the identification passes through a range of scales from the land-

---

2 Richard Long, *Selected Statements & Interviews*, London: Haunch of Venison, 2007, p. 18.

3 Gaston Bachelard, *The Poetics of Space*, New York: Penguin Books, 2014, p. 59.

4 Andrea Wulf, *The Invention of Nature, Alexander Von Humboldt's New World*, New York: Vintage Books, 2016, p. 278.

5 Christian Norberg-Schulz, *op. cit.*, p. 16.

scape right down to the smallest detail. Seen from this perspective, the house anchors the living framework, extending beyond a mere artifact that suggests (or indeed imposes) a lifestyle. (*Fig. 06*)

Based on our experience with Equis House, we used the platform and enclosure to create this living framework in our subsequent projects on the same bay. (*Fig. 07*) The platform's horizontality makes it usable for daily activities, and beneath it are the bedrooms, which require greater privacy. The enclosure demarcates a section of the desert, and seeks the necessary living space within the overwhelmingly immense landscape. But at the same time it does not try to ignore this immensity, as it relates vertically to the sky and horizontally to the ocean.

Next to Equis House, the Turrell Museum posed a different kind of challenge as a space that is not primarily domestic. Soon after opening our studio in Lima, in 2006, the owner of Equis House contacted us again, this time with a commission for a separate extension to display five light installations and a skyspace, complemented by a residence for artists. Although the platform and enclosure strategies remain valid, the most important program, in this case, would exist beneath the platform, where the artworks would be installed in the necessary darkness. Instead of galleries lined along a corridor, as initially proposed by the artist (whom we visited at his Arizona studio with our client), we suggested a circuit that began on one side of the platform, underneath the residence's vertical volume, and then descended along ramps down into the darkness, gradually accustoming the visitors' eyes to the dark before they would enter a labyrinthine space reminiscent of the Puruchuco Palace. (*Fig. 08*) The light installations would be placed within this maze of connected rooms that ultimately led to the skyspace, shifting toward natural light and ascending ramps at the other end of the platform. This project presented us with the challenge of reconciling the maze-like pre-Columbian space with the fluid space of modernity that we had begun to explore in a church for the Santa Cruz de Asia community, one of the first projects we undertook after setting up office in Lima. (*Fig. 09*) In the Turrell Museum, ramps belong to both spatial systems, acting as a ceremonial route and as a *promenade architecturale*. (*Fig. 10*)

We refined, corrected and adapted all of these reflections and hypotheses in our other projects in the same bay (the Vedoble Houses) and elsewhere (such as the Paracas Museum, the Place of Remembrance, and the faculty offices and lecture halls in the University of Piura. Equis House and the Turrell Museum began what we called "the laboratory of the patient search", which would provide the basis—initially without a roadmap as such—for a series of projects that were interconnected, and resulting project research themes which are the focus of these five chapters.

Vedoble Houses

Location
La Escondida Beach,
Cañete, Peru

Schedule
PROJECT June 2007 — June 2010
WORK May 2008 — January 2011

Lot Areas
4 x 280 m²

Floor Areas
917 m²
W1 = 255 m²
W2 = 172 m²
W3 = 217 m²
W4 = 273 m²

Design Team
Vahl del Solar
Rosa Aguirre

Construction
Modutec SAC

Structural Engineering
Luis Flores

The Vedoble Houses built on the lessons learned in our first Peruvian houses. Rather than the result of a single commission, they are a series of six, semi-detached residences built on neighboring plots between 2007 and 2013. By deciding to make Equis House not only a prototype of our research into the desert landscape but also an active hypothesis for subsequent projects, we created a compact and coherent whole. Each one forms part of a research laboratory that explores how these hypotheses are applied in response to the specific requirements of each owner and the geometry of the plot. Four constants can clearly be identified in the series:

- The *enclosure* demarcating the buildable area according to local construction codes, is handled as abstractly and "silently" as possible. From a distance it looks like an extrusion of the desert itself. An almost-imperceptible perforation marks the threshold joining and separating two exterior spaces: the infinite desert space (the "outdoor-exterior") and the private space inside the house (the "indoor-exterior"). The enclosure becomes a border around the swimming pool to set up a visual connection between the "indoor-exterior" and the ocean.

- The *artificial beach* constitutes the microcosm associated with the platform and the swimming pool, and marks the boundary between the dwelling space and the ocean landscape. The swimming pool brings the ocean into the privacy of the enclosure. In some cases it encompasses a part of the desert that accentuates its quality as a "beach" and its exterior space. Together, the different "artificial beaches" are interconnected through their swimming pools, conceived as recreational spaces where occupants can relate to each other.

- The *living-space platform* is revealed by the plot's natural slope and contains the bedrooms. The living areas were created by subtracting matter. The suspended swimming pool volume protects the bedrooms from the glare of the afternoon sun. On their lower level, the various living-space platforms are joined together by patios and corridors, connecting them like cracks in the sandy subsoil.

- The *stairs*, an open space also hewn out of the platform, link the artificial beach with the bedroom level, framing the landscape and revealing, within the complex, the plot's natural slope. This is the element that articulates the plan at the same time forms a vertical space in section.

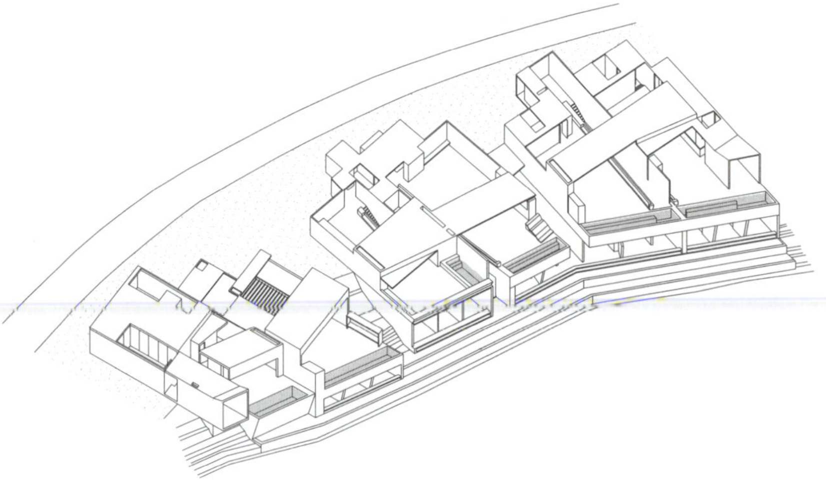

0 10

Upper floor plan Section
Ground floor plan

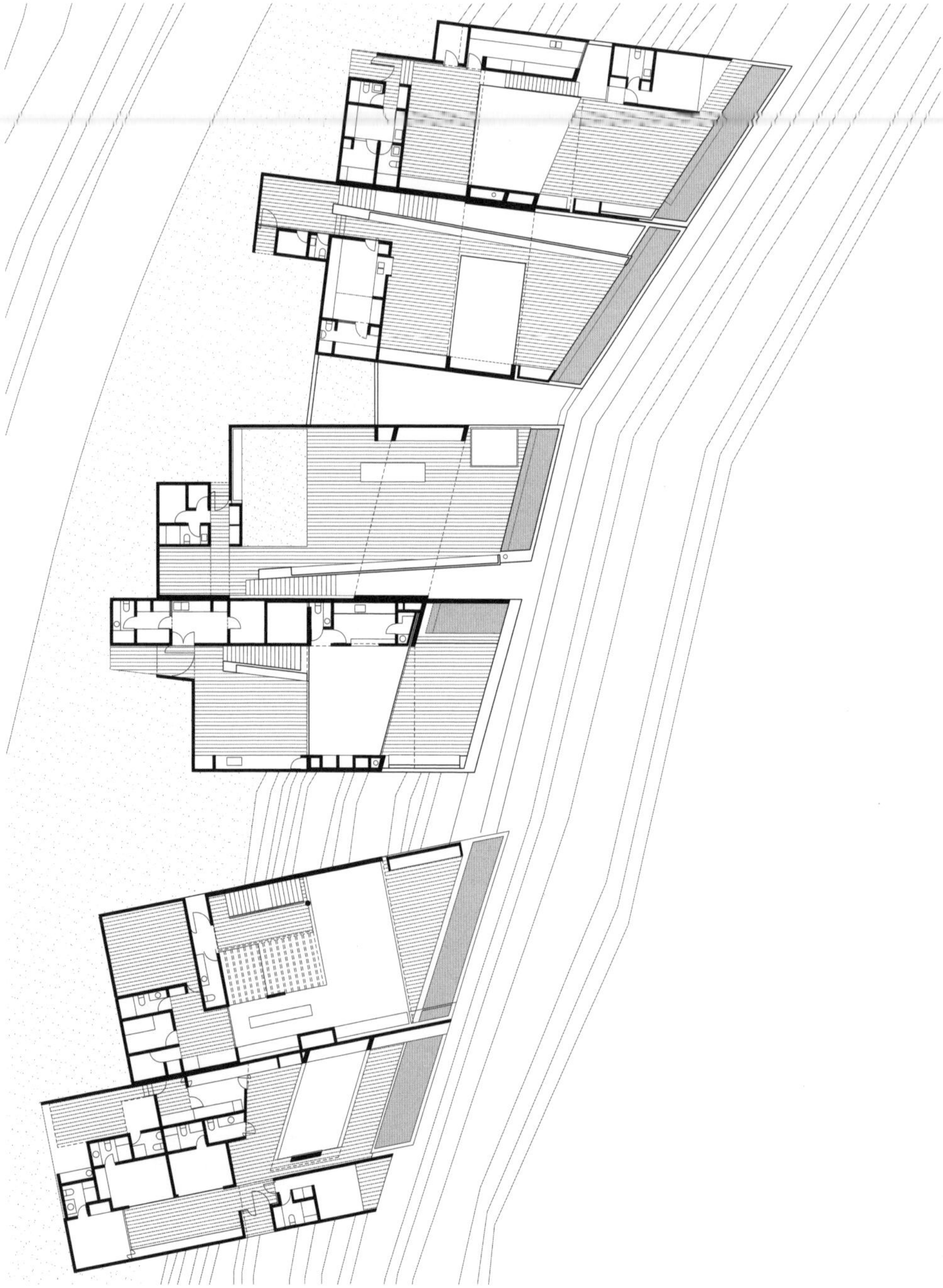

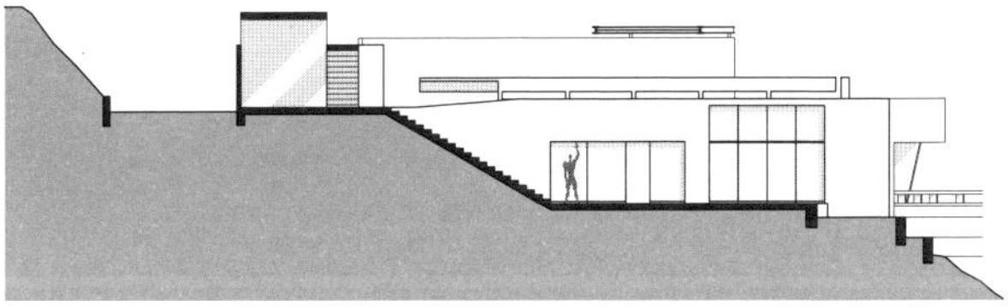

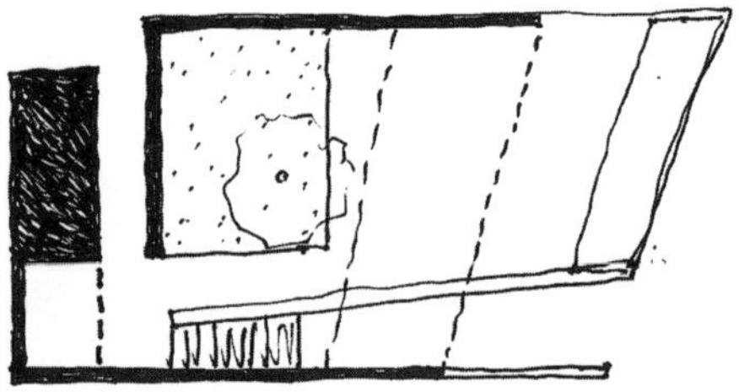

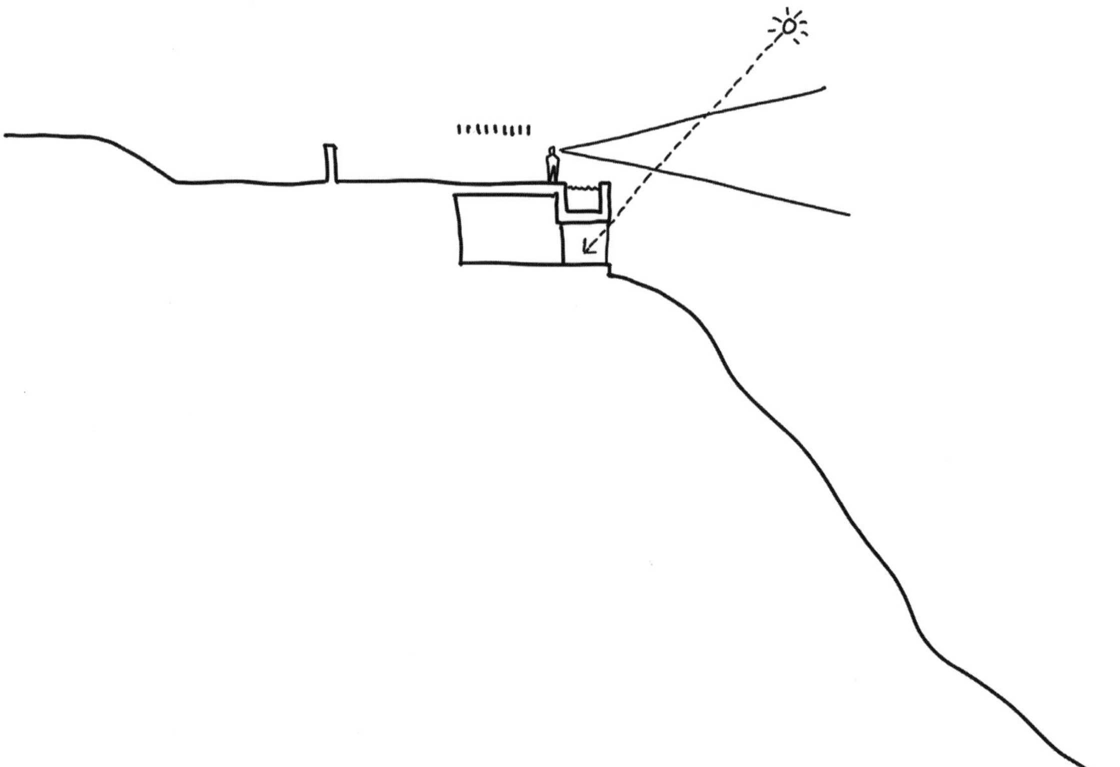

Huayoccari House

Location
Huayoccari, Cusco, Peru

Schedule
PROJECT November 2014 — July 2016
WORK July 2016 — December 2018

Lot Area
975 m^2

Floor Area
245 m^2

Design Team
Tommaso Cigarini
Andrea Otero

Structural Engineering
Jorge Indacochea

Construction
Fernando Parra

While the Vedoble Houses provided our first landscape laboratory and created a microcosm, Casa Huayoccari gave us the opportunity to continue reflecting on these themes in a very different context to the desert coast. The project comprises "twin," semi-detached houses that create a coherent and monolithic whole, as if one single construction. Ultimately only one was built.

Cusco's Urubamba valley is notable for its many snowy peaks, considered sacred by the Inca. One of these mountains, Pitusiray, looms over Huayoccari, where the house is located, at an altitude of 2,950 meters.

The house takes its cue from the surrounding mountains rather than the traditional architecture in the valley. We worked on two core elements—the ground and the roof—to create a microcosm, a small inhabited mountain, mirroring the ones that form the cultural landscape passed down to us.

The sloping ground is modified by the same feature that has historically defined Cusco's landscape: the Inca's system of agricultural terraces, in this case built using andesite, the dark red volcanic stone that give the local mountains their special hue. One of these terraces is widened to create a platform for the living space.

The classic gabled roof is disaggregated into two parts and the sloping planes are staggered to reflect the geographical context and to provide the necessary spatial and environmental conditions for creating a dwelling. The roof reflects the pitch and matter of the surrounding mountains, creating spatial compressions that frame the valley below and expanding spatially to open up toward the Incas' sacred snowy peak, the Pitusiray. The roof becomes the threshold between the horizontality of the planted fields in the valley below, and the verticality of the mountains.

Their slope also enables passive thermal regulation inside the house: the first rays of sunlight strike the roof's inner surface to warm up the living areas at dawn, while the exposed concrete and stone roof protects the house from the strong afternoon sunlight. Thermal Inertia makes it possible for the accumulated heat to radiate during the cold nights in this Quechua region.

Between the roof and the ground, solid andesite walls hide the concrete structure to join the roof to the terraces, and to create a patio that give pride of place to the sacred peak and a *pisonay*, the most important and majestic tree to grow in the central Andean region.

0 10

Ground floor plan
A-A Section
B-B Section
Upper floor plan
Axonometric

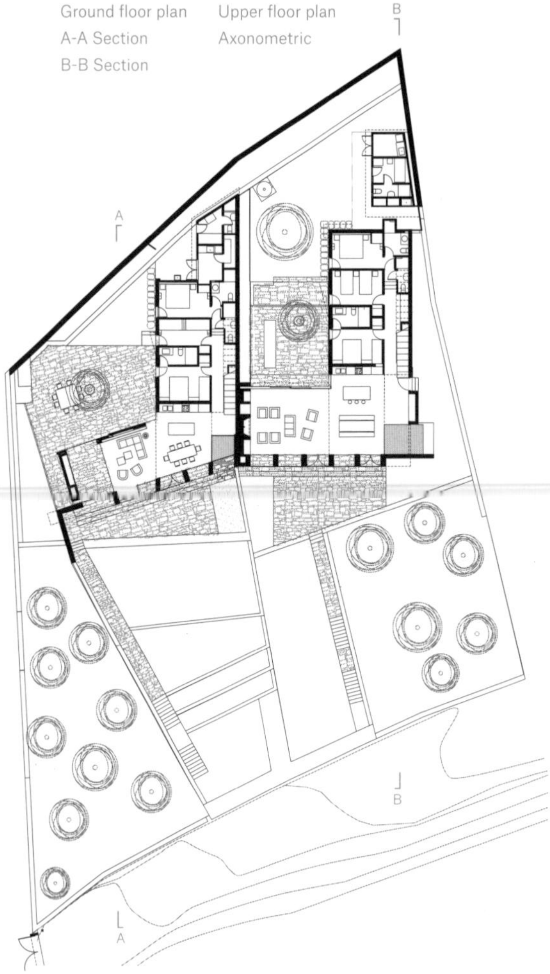

0 5

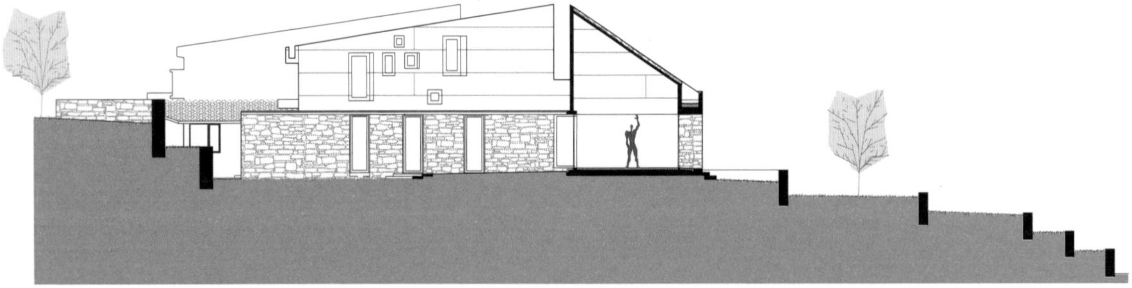

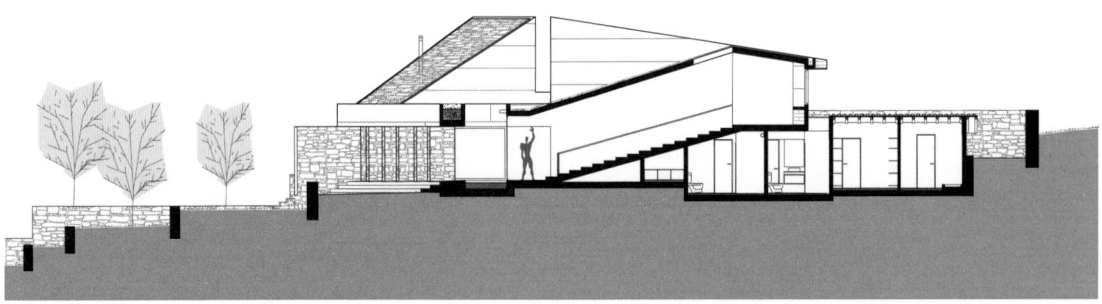

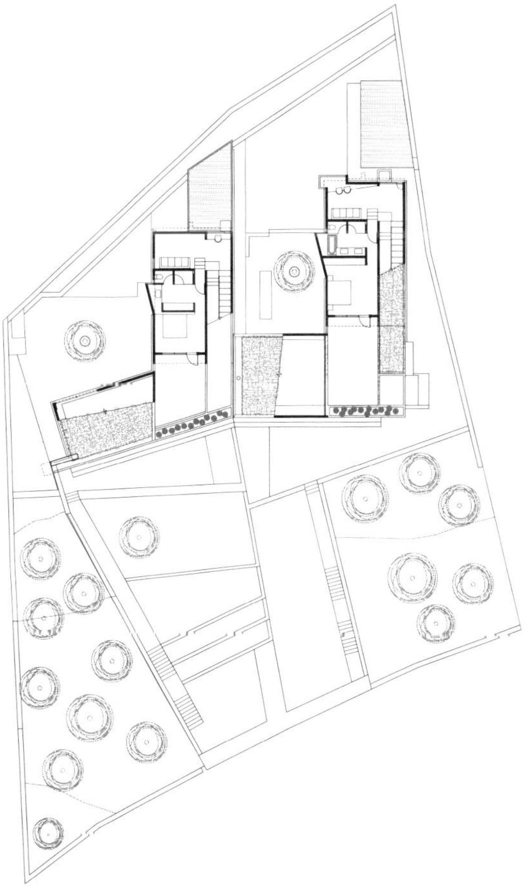

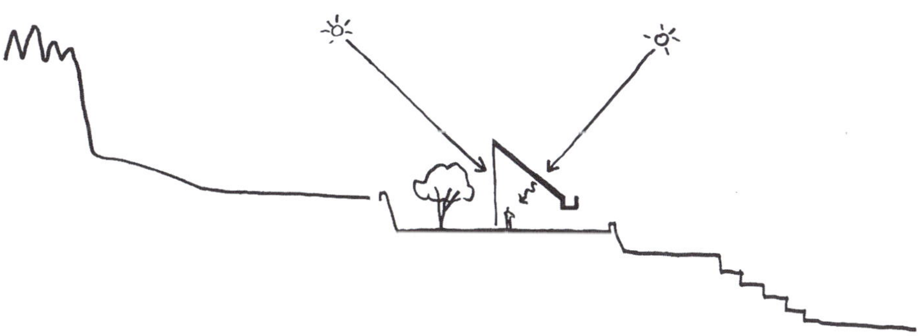

Fig. 02. Santa Cruz de Asia Church, section

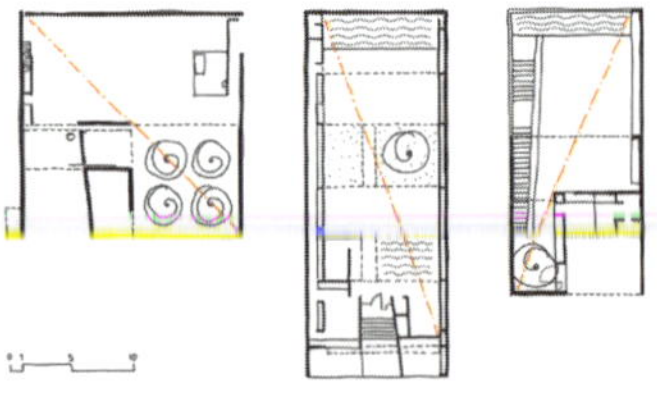

Fig. 06. Santa Cruz de Asia Church, A4 House, Equis House, spatial diagonals

Fig. 01. Equis House

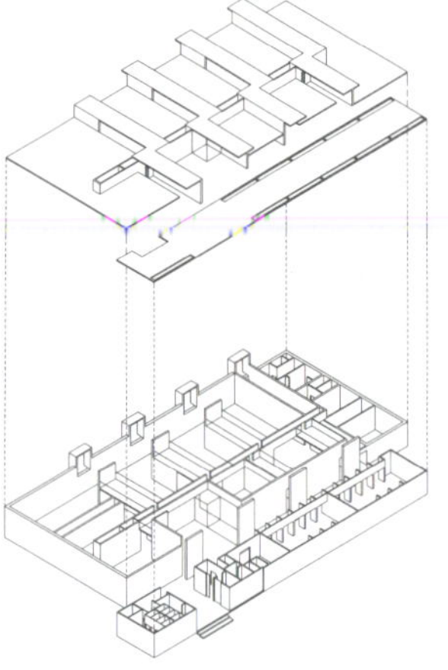

Fig. 07. Paracas Museum, axonometric

Fig. 03. Santa Cruz de Asia Church, photomontage over model

Fig. 04. Santa Cruz de Asia Church, photomontage over model

Fig. 05. Santa Cruz de Asia Church, photomontage over model

In Europe one of the paradigms of modernity was to merge indoor and exterior spaces using available technology, knocking down the visual barriers between them by adding large glazed openings and introducing fluid space as well as literal and phenomenal transparency. In tropical countries, mild climates often make it possible to explore this premise largely without requiring cutting-edge technologies and at no extra cost. Our journeys to India in 2013 and in 2017 were important in confirming our intuition: the direct connection between climate and the vast possibilities contemporary architecture can offer. In "A Place in the Sun", Charles Correa celebrates the wealth of possibilities created in this exterior-interior transition:

> In the northern regions, where the cold is severe, the architect has perforce to stay within the design parameters of a totally insulated, weather-resistant box [...]. Inside and outside exists as opposites, in a simplistic duality [...]. Compare this to the complex manifestations of built-form in a warm climate. Between the closed box and open-to-sky space there lies a whole continuum of zones with varying definitions, and degrees of protection.[1]

In 2006, a few years earlier, we designed the first project of our new studio in Lima: a church for the Santa Cruz de Asia community, commissioned by the master builder Velázques, a community leader and the person tasked with the construction of Equis House some years earlier. For this project we explored the blurring of indoor and outdoor spaces. Although it remained unbuilt, it became an essential reference point for our later work with the erasing of interior-exterior boundaries. In Equis House, the shade-providing roof was already linked to the exterior through panes of frameless, sliding tempered glass partitions that seamlessly connected the shaded space and the artificial beach. Without the need for a hermetic seal to protect from wind and rain, or for any heating or air-conditioning devices, we could limit ourselves to this delicate glazing. (*Fig. 01*)

For the church we wanted to explore further, and the nave flows into the outdoor area planted with trees, free of any obstruction between the two spaces. As an outside area yet with some indoor characteristics, the trees planted in a paved surface and surrounded by walls produced a certain ambiguity: seen from the nave, it's hard to tell whether this grove of trees, enclosed by high walls, is in fact outside or simply a continuation of the nave. From the outset, we were reluctant to call this space a courtyard, a word that conveys the idea of an outdoor space with living areas ranged around it; for us, it was more like a *hortus conclusus*, a microcosm of nature, without becoming an actual garden. (*Fig. 02*)

These ideas evolved from a conversation with Don Velázques and other leaders about what it meant to build a church in the middle of the desert. According to the Bible, deserts are synonymous with the absence of life, so the church would provide a sanctuary for divine creation. Vegetation would be represented by the four trees; animals, symbolized by the birds that would nest in them; and human beings,

Sandra Barclay
Jean Pierre Crousse

1 Charles Correa, "A Place in the Sun," *Places 1* (1), 1983, pp. 40-41.

congregated in the nave, would be welcome and present on an equal basis in the house of God. (*Fig. 03*)

In this microcosm, the sky loses its depth and is given the flatness of space. With clearly defined boundaries, the nave reinforces its interiority, yet is an exterior at the same time. As it is an equatorial region, the sun rises almost vertically. Therefore the nave's east-west orientation—following the canon of Christian religious buildings—is effective in protecting churchgoers from the sun's glare during services.

For this project, removing barriers creates an ambiguity between these two categories of space: the interior has an outdoor feel, fluidly interacting with the exterior, which has an indoor quality. (*Fig. 04*)

We should also mention the separation between the vast outside space, the landscape, and the well-ordered interior. The ambiguity only happens inside, but it is not the enclosure that defines the ambiguous spatial quality. In "Voids" at the 15th Architecture Exhibition at the Venice Biennial, the Aires Mateus brothers refer to space as "a void, a pocket of air that must be contained to define a boundary"; it's not the border itself that defines the reality of the space. In our case, the contained space clearly defines the "outside" (what does not belong to the private space) yet the "inside" (the nave and tree area) leaves an ambiguous relationship between its condition as an indoor or outdoor space. (*Fig. 05*)

Robert McCarter discusses ambiguous space in *The Space Within*. He considers it a category of space explored in modernity and associates it with cognitive experience. He quotes Semir Zeki, who writes in "The Neurology of Ambiguity" that "in cognition, the human brain tends to spend little time or cognitive energy on easily categorized or familiar events, and instead is engaged and challenged by events or elements that have multiple, equally valid meanings or interpretations, including learning, judgement, memory and experience."[2] Richard Sennett reinforces this concept, arguing that "planned ambiguity acquires more value if the designer intends that others learn something from momentary disorientation, become skilled in dealing with ambiguity" and he relates ambiguity to the economy of means, considering that "creating ambiguity as a special instance of applying minimum force."[3]

Involving and challenging cognition through ambiguous categories has been a constant area of exploration in our work, and is visible to varying degrees depending on the particular circumstances of our commissions. Again, in mild, tropical climates this ambiguity does not require overdetermination or any extra effort. Overdetermined spaces in buildings that are precisely defined in terms of their program or function swiftly become obsolete, insofar as uses change over time. Precision understood as a part of a project does not exclude ambiguity, opening up the door to unexpected uses.

Our design for the Turrell Museum included an outdoor labyrinthine route underneath a roof and with interior spatial qualities. This is a "continuation of the outdoors," whose ambiguity is modulated

---

2 Robert McCarter, *The Space Between: Interior Experience as the Origin of Architecture*, London: Reaktion Books, 2016, p. 99.

3 Richard Sennett, *The Craftsman*, New Haven: Yale University Press, 2008, pp. 233-234.

by luminous intensity. In the Paracas Museum, although the need to conserve the work on display makes it necessary to close the exhibition galleries and isolate them from the rest of the building, the spaces that connect the program's various elements are exterior spaces with an indoor feel, are the "indoor-exteriors."

In much of our work, spaces are intersected by an obstacle-free diagonal, making it possible to "size up" the longest distance between the boundaries, whether within an enclosure or the edges of the plot. This unobstructed diagonal crosses both exterior and interior space without distinction, making it possible to merge the boundaries between both and giving people the impression that the space is larger than it actually is. (*Fig. 06*) This strategy of using an unobstructed diagonal was inspired by Henri Ciriani, our teacher and mentor, who has a vast knowledge of architectural space, who describes it as "expanding space." We believe that "diagonal space" is so important because it can help explain one of the defining characteristics of Corbusier's "inexpressible space." In *Modulor 2*, Le Corbusier states—without specifying that it is owing to the spatial diagonal—that "a fathomless depth gapes open, all walls are broken down, every other presence is put to flight, and the miracle of *inexpressible* space is achieved..."[4] The "inexpressible space" is the space that is exciting because of its set of proportions, materiality, light and the actual qualities of space, although he never explained how to achieve it.

In the Paracas Museum's exhibition galleries we explored another category of space, one that what we called "suggested space." We refer to the space that is fluid as observers shift position, where time actively intervenes and reconfigures the spatial expanse in the mind, without requiring an obstacle-free diagonal. This means that a certain space—which can also conform to the labyrinth's planimetric layout—can also expand and create depths thanks to those suggested spaces that are not perceived but sensed by small transparencies due to the presence of light shining from a hidden source or from other devices within the project to encourage visitors to explore and discover them. (*Fig. 07*)

The two projects described below have pushed the envelope in our work. The first one is a city residence in Lima that combines spatial expansion with a linear and ambiguous series of open and roofed spaces, where we explore the idea of the "indoor-exterior" which we will see in more detail in the following chapter. In the second one, a restaurant also in Lima, explores the possibility of developing a hybrid between a courtyard (a type of space that usually prevents spatial expansion) and the unobstructed diagonal.

4 Le Corbusier, *The Modulor and Modulor 2*, trans. Peter de Francia and Anna Bostock, Basel: Birkhäuser, 2015, p. 27.

A4 House

Location
San Isidro, Lima, Peru

Schedule
PROJECT January 2012 — December 2013
WORK March 2014 — June 2016

Lot Area
564 m²

Floor Area
1,042 m²

Design Team
Martín Montañez
Fernando Quiñones

Structural Engineering
Jorge Indacochea

Construction
Yuri Bustios

This house heightens the contrast between its daily living spaces and the private bedroom areas, similarly to the Vedoble and Equis houses, only here in an urban context and as a primary residence. This is a typical urban lot—with a frontage of 15 meters and a depth of 38 meters—surrounded by two-story properties.

We chose an introspective layout, making the most of local building regulations which require plots to be surrounded by four-meter-high walls. We heightened this introvertedness by adding few openings onto the street, taking our cue from pre-Hispanic and colonial traditions. We recreated an indoor landscape within the enclosure, and developed a living area on one, continuous space, the size of the plot. This starts at the entrance, raised 1.5 meters above street level, with a series of elements defining the ground level's features: a reflecting pool, courtyard, a tree-filled garden, and a swimming pool with a sun deck.

Unlike our beach houses with their bedroom areas located beneath the platform, in this residence we placed them on the second floor, distributed across three domed bridges supported by the perimeter walls. These bridges define a sequence of three roofed spaces and three open spaces, four of them outside and two that can be closed with sliding glass doors, defining its ambiguous quality.

The duality between the social space and the garden is erased by this unique space contained and given rhythm by the bridges and the celestial vault. The spatial expanse produced by the unobstructed diagonal is connected to the concatenation of spaces. In this case, the depth of the series emphasizes the ambiguity within the continuity.

One side of the lot has a servant space that provides functional continuity to every enclosure, both on the social and on the private floor—where the volumes supported by the vaulted bridges are essentially opaque, marked by extruded volumes that allow light to enter and offer a cozy space for reading and resting in the bedrooms. The bridges are joined by two metal walkways open to the tree-filled garden and a reflecting pool that contrast with the volumes' opacity.

0 5

Section

Upper floor plan

Ground floor plan

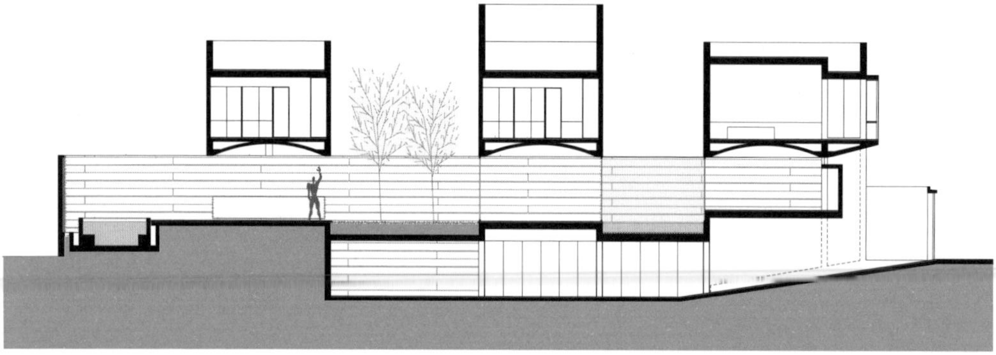

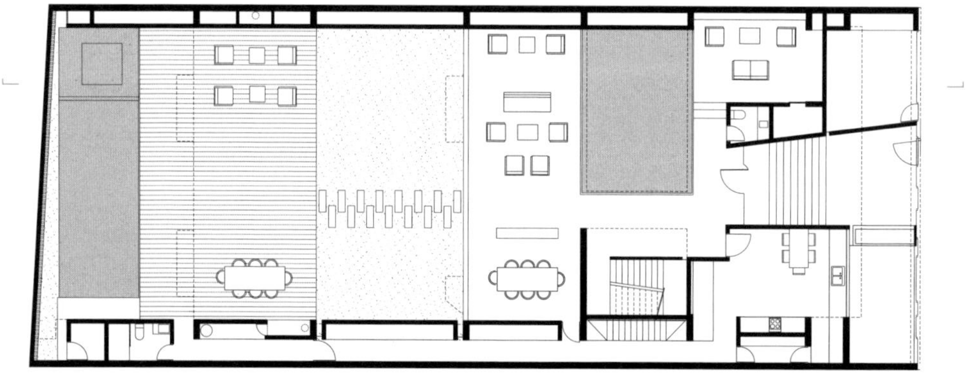

Limaná Restaurant

Location
San Isidro, Lima, Peru

Schedule
PROJECT March – December 2018
WORK January – November 2019

Lot Area
741 m²

Floor Area
413 m²

Client
Grupo Crosland

Project Manager
Andrea Otero

Structural Engineering
Jorge Avendaño

Construction
KAM SAU SAC

The commission was to create a restaurant to represent Lima's uniqueness, with elements that could be replicated in other establishments. Our view is that these aspects should focus on the spatial conditions created by Lima's unique climate, the typical introspection of colonial and pre-Hispanic residences, and the regulation of the interior lighting conditions.

The University of Piura's lecture halls and faculty office building, completed one year previously, had a direct impact on this project: a citadel of functional buildings that create intermediate spaces between them.

We began by creating a 6-meter-wide, 5.4-meter-tall module for several functions that received purely overhead natural lighting and ventilation, to set up an unobstructed connection with other modules on a horizontal plane and to create a constant spatial fluidity between them. In this module, the first 2.1 meters from the ground are open, with a bare minimum of supporting structures, and the next 3.3 meters are opaque, crowned by a 2.6-meter-high skylight. The 2.1 meter height also defines that of the enclosure, which acts as a belt connecting the various modules.

At the project's specific location we created an inner world with five modules forming an intermediate space. A large, fluid space emerges at eye level, similar to the living area in the A4 House. The intermediate space is alternately compressed and expanded by the asymmetry of these modules, producing the quality of an indoor space despite being an open-air, exterior area. Its dimensions are similar to those of the module, so that the whole appears as a concatenation of roofed and open environments—all of which are exterior—yet in which everything is perceived to be "indoors," whether under a roof or in the open air.

Each module has a differentiated use and a way of experiencing the act of eating in a restaurant: the first comprises a food store and areas for eating a quick snack, the second is furnished with long tables for a communal eating experience, the third has a more classic arrangement of individual tables for up to four diners, the fourth has a bar and high tables with stools, and the fifth is a private space separated from the other areas. Depending on the time of day, some modules are busier than others, while the intermediate spaces articulate these distinctions with tables and chairs.

Placer
sin culpa

0 10

Section

Upper floor plan

Ground floor plan

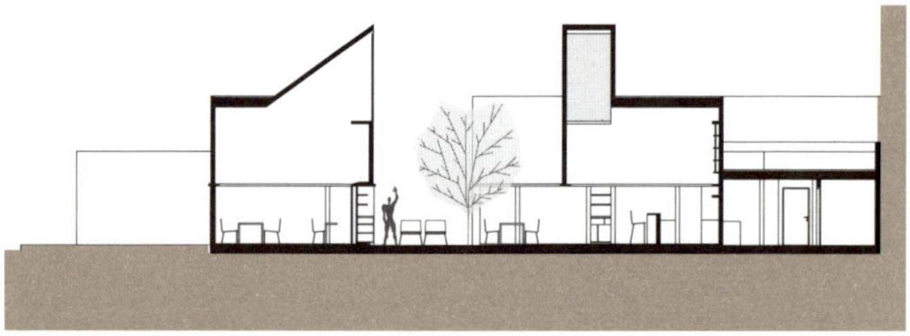

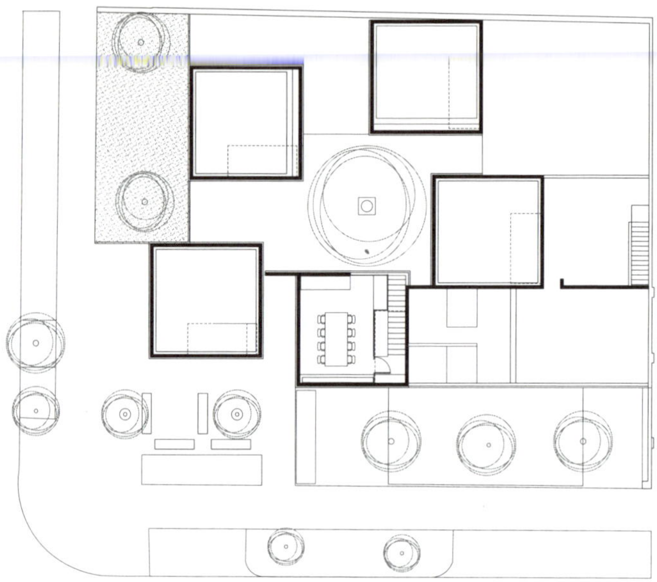

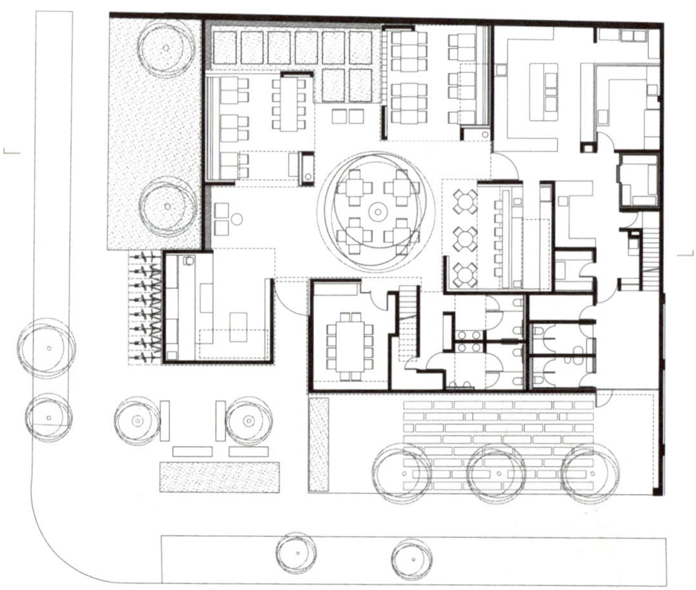

LIMANÁ CAFÉ

MANÁ BAR

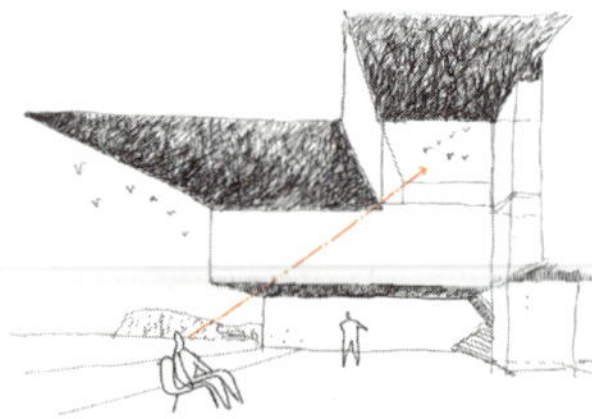

Fig. 06. M6 House, sketch

Fig. 08. University of Piura's lecture halls under construction

Fig. 07. Moquegua Regional Government's Offices

Fig. 04. Visual Arts School, model

Fig. 03. Vedoble Houses

Figs. 01 and 02. Mill Owners' Association Building, visit photographs

Fig. 05. Visual Arts School

Indoor Exteriors

> It may seem paradoxical at first mention, but the interior experience of the exterior environment is a critical aspect of this conception of interior primacy in architecture. Architects whose interior spaces remain in our memory have invariably been acutely sensitive to the local climate, the constant change of the seasons and natural light, and the larger environment in which the building is placed, and how these may be engaged to enrich the experience of the inhabitants in the space within.[1]

Robert McCarter's description of the "space within" seems like an argument in favor of bioclimatic architecture, but it describes something that should really be commonplace in countries with tropical climates.

Experiencing the outdoors as an interior has always appealed to us, and working in Peru has brought this into sharper focus. We have built the vast majority of our projects in environments that have helped us understand exterior, interior, inside, and outside spaces as mutually independent. If we understand the interior-exterior duality as the dichotomy between physical shelter and insulation, as opposed to the lack of such protection, then the inside-outside duality relates, by contrast, to a phenomenological condition of feeling outside or inside a contained space.

When thanks to a benign climate architecture no longer needs to offer shelter, its active role in terms of space, materiality, and time releases the exterior from being architecturally synonymous with the "outdoors" and the interior from being "indoors." This is not necessarily about creating ambiguous spaces, as we saw in the previous chapter. Some of our projects do not explore this ambiguity but instead draw a clear line between outdoor and indoor spaces, interiors and exteriors. The indoor-exterior binomial has always been the most intriguing one for us—that sensation of being in an outside space yet one with interior qualities.

From the time we saw it in books, Le Corbusier's Ahmedabad Textile Mill Owners' Association House (ATMA House) impressed us greatly by revealing the importance of space in architecture. On our first trip to India in 2012, Le Corbusier and Kahn's work revealed the possibilities open to us in Peru; visiting it was a seminal moment in our quest to bring the outside indoors. (*Fig. 01*) After entering via the ramp, crossing the threshold of the brise-soleils gives the sensation of being in a space that boasts this quality. Despite its apparent compactness when viewed from outside, the exterior penetrates inside the building's three main floors, in a space contained by the brise-soleils yet expanding beyond them. Volumes that seem to be buildings inhabit this indoor-exterior, which in turn transform it into a landscape in its own right. (*Fig. 02*) A similar phenomenon can be observed in Curutchet House, another of our architectural reference points, although in this case the indoor-exterior is more clearly connected to the *promenade architecturale*.

This interest in creating indoor-exterior landscapes has constantly guided our projects, from our first summer houses to the University of Piura's lecture theaters and faculty offices.

Sandra Barclay
Jean Pierre Crousse

1 Robert McCarter, *The Space Between: Interior Experience as the Origin of Architecture*, London: Reaktion Books, 2016, p. 129.

The dichotomies of interior/exterior, compact/fluid and free/confined are a vein running through our work, although it was only relatively recently that we became conscious of this. The outer appearances of the buildings included in this book are always opaque, with a simple and often unobtrusive geometry, rooted in the ground. The entrance always signals the threshold in which this reality leads to a complex spatial quality, to a celebration of the exterior as the new interior and the creation of landscapes through the "populating" of this space with objects—furniture or buildings—that create hierarchies between what is close, what is distant, the foreground and the horizon. (*Fig. 03*) The indoor-exterior is the space in which the body, the eye and the light move independently though space and time on both the horizontal and vertical plane.

This obsession has even infused projects that might initially seem ill-suited to such an approach. For example, it can be found in our vertical extension of the former home of architect Emilio Harth Terré, which was declared a national heritage site and had recently been converted into a visual arts school. The house's shallow volumes were arranged around a courtyard, creating the need for a connection through the courtyard to the teaching spaces to be added on top of the house. Based on the metal structure and components—required in order to build on top of the existing building—we chose to extend the courtyard space and insert a helix of transparent walkways like suspended courtyards to create places for casual learning encounters in the spaces between the traditional courtyard and the accessible rooftop. The new proportions of the courtyard create an outdoor room, with workshops and classrooms attached to it. (*Figs. 04 and 05*)

In M6 House, the indoor-exterior also creates an eminently vertical space, except in this case by opening up horizontally toward the ocean. Working with transparencies and visual diagonals, we were able to strike a balance between this powerful frame and the visual clarity toward the sky and the street to maintain the necessary feeling of being inside, and its "indoor" quality. (*Fig. 06*). In doing so, we generated a spatial diagonal that is no longer expressed in the plan but in the section, becoming an "oblique."

Shortly after completing M6 House, we participated in an invitational competition to design the Moquegua regional government's new headquarters, our largest non-residential project to date. Positioned at the edge of the Atacama desert, near the Chilean border, we decided to explore the possibility of creating an indoor-exterior constituted by the space between the functional buildings required by the program. Six buildings in close proximity to one another create long and narrow courtyards, oriented to regulate solar gain. The courtyards are connected by a large indoor-exterior space connected to the entrance lobby as well as to the threshold connecting the outdoor-exterior and the indoor-exterior. This threshold is a shady space accessible to all citizens, articulating the administrative spaces around an urban plaza, a powerful image for a regional government that aspires to be inclusive and generous with the citizens of Moquegua. (*Fig. 07*)

The university building in Piura, designed while the regional government headquarters was under construction, is the site of our most complex indoor-exterior space. Without the imposition of any specific programmatic requirement, this space becomes a place for informal learning, prioritizing casual encounters between students, and between students and faculty members. It is modulated by spaces with varying levels of privacy, encouraging study and the exchange of ideas outside the formal classroom setting. For this project we revisited the idea of buildings separated by the indoor-exterior, but in this case the separation is complete. Each one of the 11 buildings has its own roof that extends until it almost touches the others, leaving slots for light to enter, shielding the interior from the direct glare of the sun. (*Fig. 08*) The separation ensures the interior and exterior spaces are well ventilated and adequately lit. This university extension was in response to the government's "Beca 18" grant that offered the chance for 700 rural state school pupils from low-income families to enroll at private universities. The indoor-exterior design, justified by the bright sunshine and heat of Peru's equatorial desert region, was also developed as a non-hierarchical space where the newly enrolled students could integrate with the existing student population outside the classroom.

The vertical campus of the University of Engineering and Technology (UTEC), in Lima, designed by Grafton Architects' Shelley McNamara and Yvonne Farrell, was particularly important for us. UTEC's monumental indoor-exterior became a unique local, contemporary reference point to prove to our clients the transcendence of this idea, and to overcome the apprehensions such "function-less" open-air spaces give rise to. In fact, in emerging countries the desire to achieve a certain level of development goes hand in hand with an appetite for and dependence on construction technologies and air conditioning systems that make no sense in our latitudes. Hermetically sealed and temperature-controlled spaces proliferate when comfortable conditions outdoors are the norm. These sophisticated technologies often distance architecture from its purpose of providing well-being, as Robert McCarter puts it so well: "we can trace a direct path from the time when human comfort depended on the intimate layer of architecture—such as St Jerome's wooden study—to the time when human comfort became almost entirely independent of it, reliant instead on the thermostat regulating the hermetically-sealed interior."[2] Tackling this phenomenon—which took 50 years to take root in other parts of the world and is now in retreat in some places—remains an exhausting, everyday struggle in Peru.

2 *Ibid.*, p. 130.

M6 House

Location
Punta Hermosa, Lima, Peru

Schedule
PROJECT March 2011 — March 2012
WORK May 2012 — March 2013

Lot Area
240 m^2

Floor Area
940 m^2

Design Team
Juan Miguel Chinchay
Alfredo Castro

Structural Engineering
Jorge Indacochea

Construction
Aceros y Concretos S.A.

This house is located in a built-up area of the Punta Hermosa beach resort, 45 kilometers south of Lima. The adjoining properties have two frontages: vehicular access is from a rear street, while pedestrians enter from an oceanfront esplanade above the narrow beach.

The design revisits the porch typology found in 19th-century beach houses, providing an intermediate space between interior and exterior. This is traditionally used as an informal social space within homes, as described by Flora Tristán in *Peregrinaciones de una paria*.[3] We decided to revive this idea, now virtually extinct, to propose a house-porch that, except for the bedrooms, would make everything an intermediate space, an indoor-exterior.

Unlike the porch, however, here the exterior enters the home and passes through the space both vertically and horizontally, maintaining a balance between the large, framed ocean views and the visual transparencies toward the sky and the street, in order to turn the entire living area into a shaded, open-air space that connects the house's three levels. This large contemporary porch itself forms an interior landscape connected to the adjacent beach and ocean, each acquiring new meanings. For this to occur, we carried out a meticulous operation in opacities and transparencies, generating a series of planes to the front, intermediate, and rear. Compensating for the pulling power of the framed ocean view, we created two spatial diagonals: one in plan forming a visual link from the beach to the entrance porch and the street to the rear, and the other in section, an "oblique" linking the lounge with the sky.

In order to enable the creation of this "indoor landscape," the maximum sizes allowed by the local building code are employed to create a parallelepiped that is then "excavated" in the design process to create living areas. The house is entirely column-free, with the partition walls forming a dual shell structure with the roof, which doubles up as a servant space to bring natural light and ventilation into all the bathrooms. The volumes containing the bedrooms are suspended over the large porch and create a continuous movement of planes that demarcate interconnected spaces and multiple sightlines inside the house.

3 Flora Tristán, *Peregrinaciones de una paria*, Lima: Terra Incógnita, 2003.

200

190

0 5

Level 2 floor plan
Level 1 floor plan
Ground floor plan

A-A Section
B-B Section

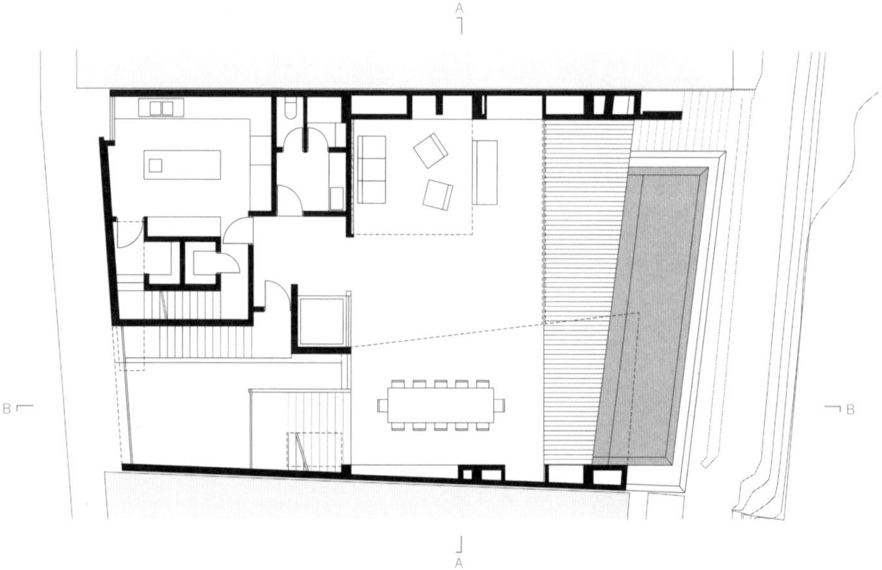

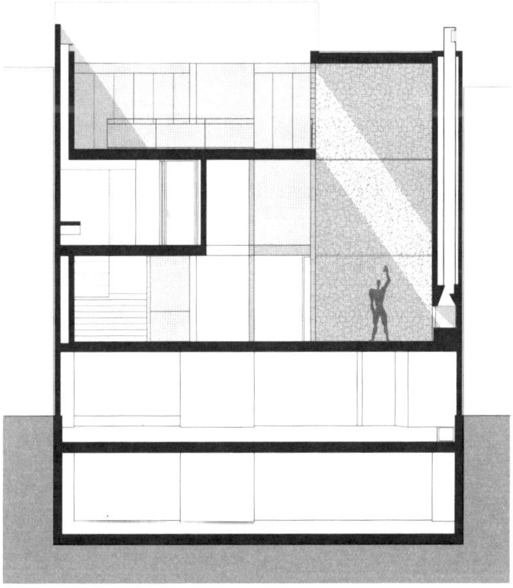

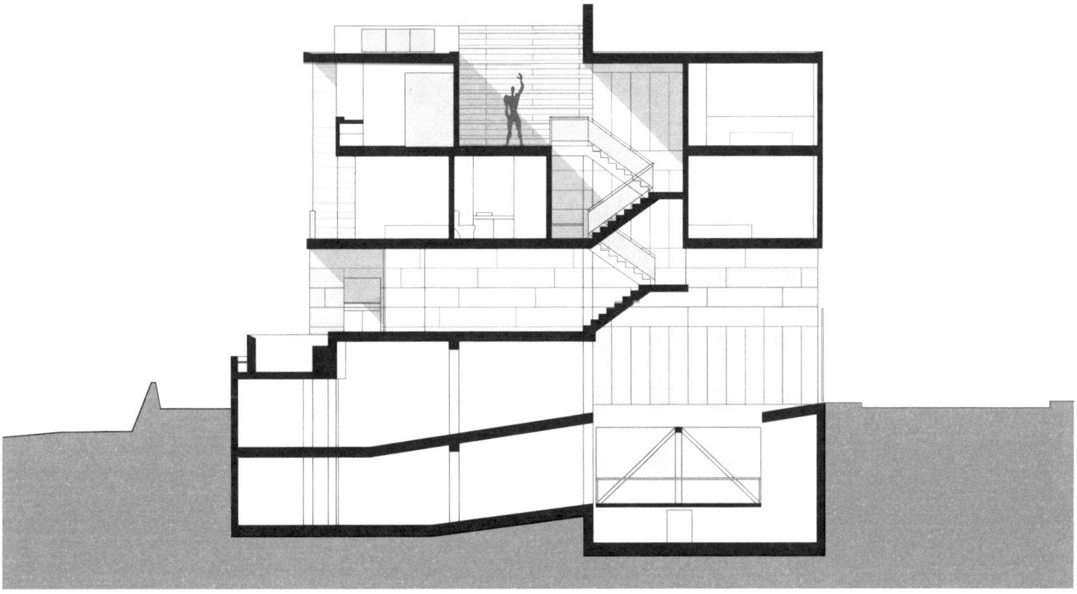

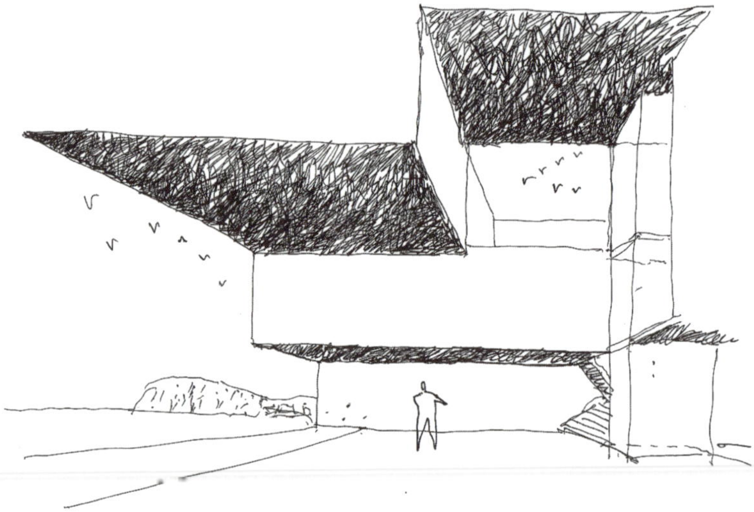

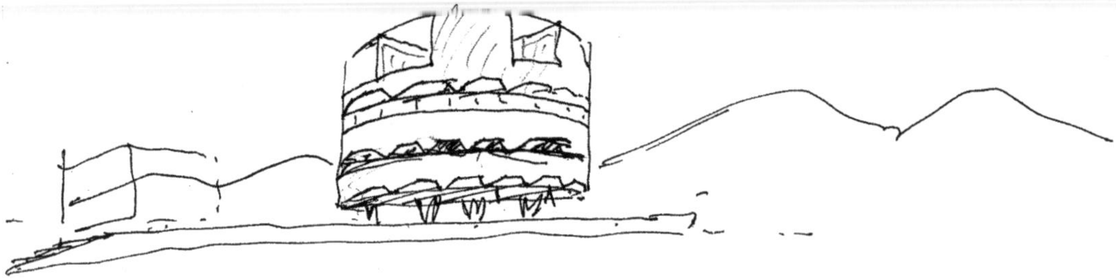

Moquegua Regional Government Offices

Location
Moquegua, Peru

Schedule
PROJECT September 2013 – December 2015
WORK April 2016 – December 2017
OPENING January 2015

Lot Area
15,605 m^2

Floor Area
14,505 m^2

Design Team
PRELIMINARY PROJECT
Eduardo Zambrano
PROJECT MANAGER
María Isabel Pineda

External Management
KUKOVA

Project Supervision and Structural Engineering
GCAQ

Sanitary Engineering
Equipo G

Electrical Engineering
AT Consultores

Mechanical Engineering
PRO TERM Perú SAC

Security Engineering
Engineering Services SAC

Lighting
Rie Sakata Lighting Designers

Acoustics
Carlos Jiménez

Environmental Conditioning
Cecilia Jiménez

Construction
INCOT Contratistas Generales

This project is part of the city of Moquegua's new urban development, a regional government initiative that includes a shopping mall, sports facilities, and a school. The new offices for the public administration required a large auditorium to make up for the lack of spaces for cultural events and for conferences in southern Peru.

Our project won the competition with its compact, six-floor design that incorporates a large, open public plaza—an element not contemplated in the competition brief. This new space provides a connection between the various parts of the new development, while the building itself has a unique appearance with a large entrance ramp, roofed public atrium, and a distinct shape within its urban surroundings.

The cylindrical outline is inspired by Moquegua's most important historical and geographical landmark, the Cerro Baúl, a mountain that was home to two great pre-Hispanic cultures, the Wari and the Tiwanaku.

While the circular perimeter shortens the evacuation routes and reduces the number of vertical circulation and service areas to two, the structure and spaces for working are orthogonal cores with a simple 7 x 7-meter grid layout. The outer ring demarcates and envelops six buildings separated by five courtyards positioned to provide the offices with natural lighting and ventilation, preventing direct sunlight and ensuring pleasant temperatures. Four of these courtyards are glazed on their north and south façades, which are almost equivalent due to the latitude, while the fifth is a roofed space, bringing together the horizontal circulations and linked to the other four.

Both the circular geometry and the orientation and layout of the courtyards generates significant efficiencies in terms of energy, circulation routes, networks and safety devices, making it possible to equip the structure with seismic dampers while remaining within the budget. As a result, these government offices can be used as a shelter in the event of a natural disaster, making the investment not only for the regional government administration but also for the entire population of the city of Moquegua.

0 15

Level 4 floor plan A-A Section
Level 3 floor plan B-B Section
Ground floor plan C-C Section

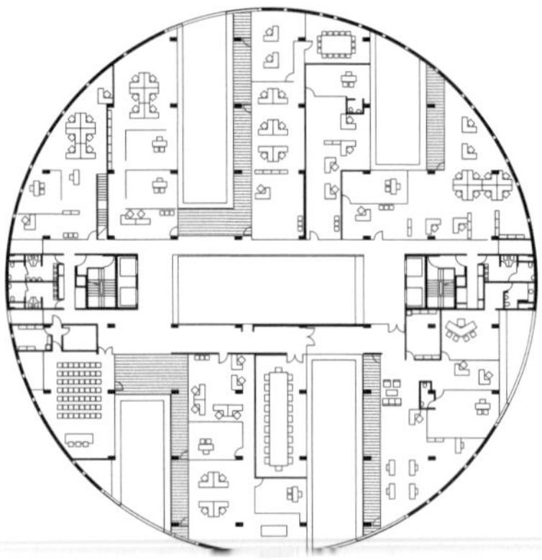

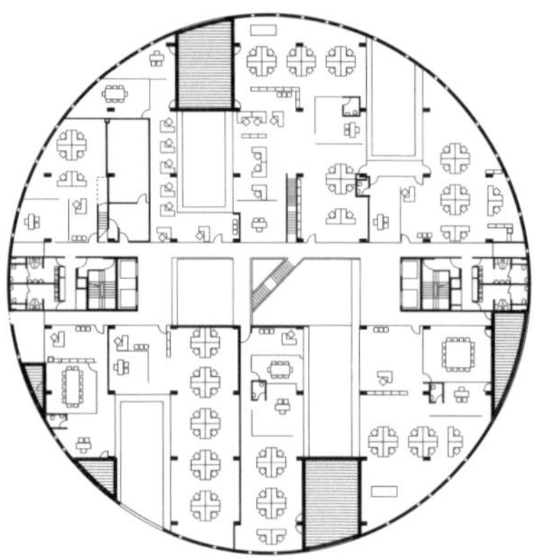

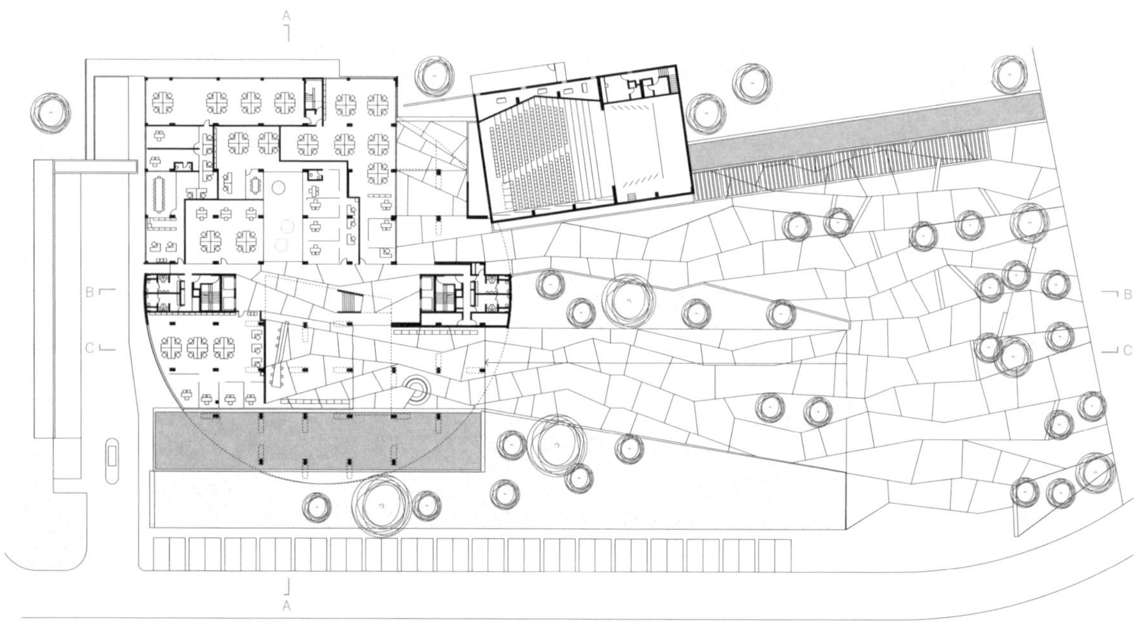

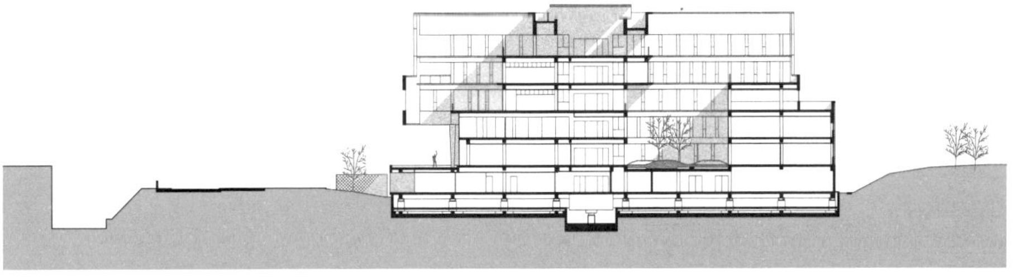

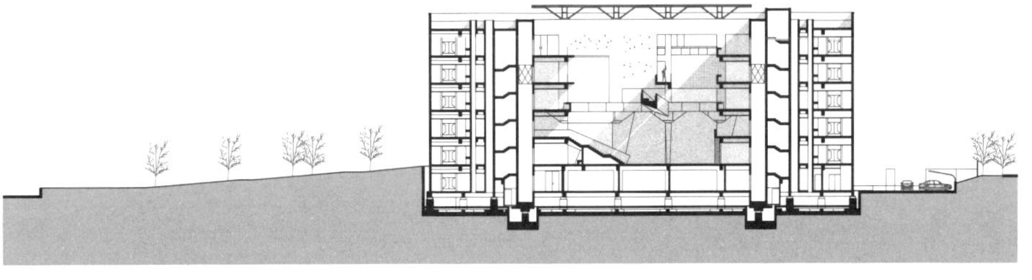

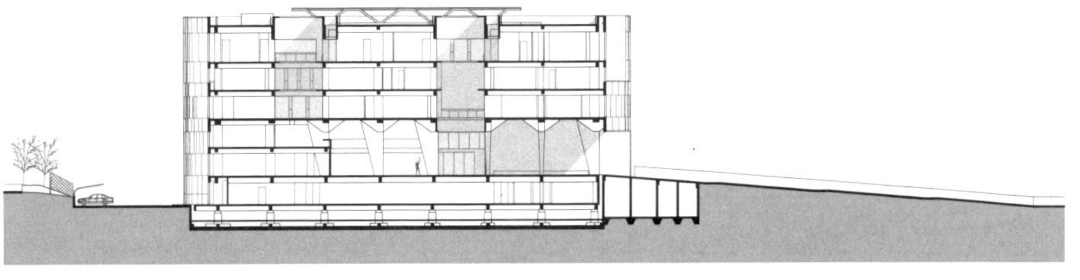

SALIDA

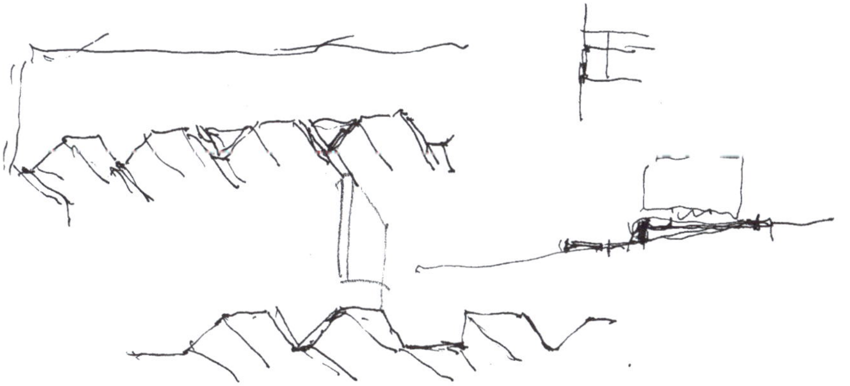

Fig. 02. Place of Remembrance, the artificial cliff

Fig. 04. Place of Remembrance, craftsmen placing boulders

Fig. 03. Place of Remembrance, artisan formwork

Fig. 01. Vedoble Houses, concrete laboratory

We found that among the most striking differences between working in France and in Peru are the methods of producing architecture and the construction processes used. In France, similarly to other industrialized countries, efficiency is prized above all else, particularly in order to safeguard the capital invested. Design schedules are shorter, materials and construction processes must meet pre-established standards, and the creative process must cease once sitework has begun, with projects overdetermined with plans and specifications.

The construction industry, together with insurance companies and technical supervisors, imposes the use of standardized construction processes and industrial materials that minimize the risks of imperfections and reduce margins of error. However, this inevitably distances the architect from the builder, and skillful construction becomes replaced by an act of assembling with a decreased involvement of expert craftmanship.

Álvaro Siza has written about the difference between building in Holland, where there is an abundance of industrial materials from which to choose, and the situation in Portugal, where there were far fewer options compared to more industrialized countries. This apparent paucity has actually allowed him to develop greater experience with fewer materials, acquiring a deeper knowledge of construction in Portugal than in Holland.

If we were to compare European and Peruvian realities, this difference becomes vast; it requires a fundamental shift in the way of imagining architecture. As we have mentioned, returning to Peru made us reconsider our approach to architecture with all the possibilities offered by the benign climate of the Peruvian coast, that we experienced in the three houses we designed in Peru while we were still based in Paris. However, simply by practicing architecture in the country, once we had moved back to Lima, we realized the importance of understanding the production methods and available technology to continue rethinking the way we design.

Our first experiences as local architects led us to ask three essential questions: How do buildings age here? How can the scarcity of resources be treated as an opportunity? Can construction processes ascribe meaning to the building itself?

David Leatherbarrow and Mohsen Mostafavi speak of ageing and wear, and ask:

> Is weathering only subtraction, can it not also *add* and enhance? Deleterious consequences can be complemented by the potential value of sedimentation and the accumulation of detritus on a surface through the action of weather [...] not to see finishing as the final moment of construction but to see the unending deterioration of a finish that results from weathering, the continuous metamorphosis of the building itself, as part of its beginning(s) and its ever-changing 'finish'.[1]

Decisions taken during the creative process and while building are clearly crucial to incorporating the life and the ageing of the building

1 David Leatherbarrow and Mohsen Mostafavi, *On Weathering. The Life of Buildings in Time*, Cambridge: MIT Press, 1993, p. 6.

into the logic of the project itself. Buildings on the coast of Peru are weathered by the vast quantities of desert dust that coat horizontal and vertical surfaces, whereas elsewhere this effect is caused by significant changes in temperature or rain—both factors that are non-existent in this region of Peru. Here, modern architecture, mainly painted in white, visually ages because of dust, requiring yearly repainting.

For our earlier projects in Peru we proposed using ocher paint to make the buildings blend into the desert, but once we had actually moved back to the country we experimented with the local craftmanship and the ability of exposed concrete to absorb this dust in our laboratory of the Vedoble houses. The handcrafted formwork is key to this material, since the roughness of the worn boards allows the dust to accumulate without creating stains. (*Fig. 01*)

In the Place of Remembrance this acquired further connotations as a result of the project's vocation to establish a geographic landmark. Conceived as an artificial outcrop to complement the cliffs and ravines along the steep-sided bay of Lima, the building had to take on the color of its surroundings, among other aspects, in order to meld into the landscape. No special aggregates or dyes were used, and the very tight budget ruled them out anyway. The solution was simply to let dust accumulate on the rough concrete finish. The passage of time—barely a couple of years—was enough for the Place of Remembrance to acquire the same color as the cliffs. (*Fig. 02*)

We repeated this strategy for the lecture halls and faculty offices at the University of Piura, located in the dry tropical forest of the northern desert, where the exterior is constructed with traditional formwork that absorbs the dust, while steel formwork was used inside to enable the required speed of construction.

Another important conclusion was the need for local construction processes to root projects in their surroundings. Peru still lacks its own construction industry yet has the advantage and freedom of drawing on skilled labor that use traditional construction technologies while coexisting with contemporary industrial technologies and materials imported from industrialized countries.

The financial constraints facing us in the public buildings constructed over the past ten years left us in no doubt that it is possible, economically viable, and even advantageous to exploit this artisanal dimension to the construction process. This is in stark contrast to Europe, where such labor is reserved for buildings with lavish budgets, and generally applies to heritage projects.

In the Place of Remembrance, thanks to the absence of draconian construction deadlines, we opted for traditional technologies that required more workers. This generated savings in the construction process, avoiding the use of a crane, and was feasible for the limited budget we were assigned. This decision introduced a modus operandi that was different to the one we were accustomed to in our French projects: the creative process was prolonged during the construction of the building and was connected to a constant dialogue with the craftsmen and builders. As Richard Sennett writes: "the laborer with a sense of craft becomes engaged in the work in and for himself; the satisfactions of working are their own reward [...] work is connected to the freedom to experiment."[2] This was demonstrated to us by those who worked on the project, and the commitment and care invested in their work, were decisive to the result. We engaged in constant conversation with builders, carpenters, and concrete specialists, in the certainty that the best result would be sought, even if not necessarily the most perfect in technical terms or the most efficient in economic ones. The concrete for the Place of Remembrance was hand-poured, with traditional formwork made from recycled boards. Concrete walls were built following the logic of rammed-earth construction, and connected with the accumulative logic of the alluvial strata of Lima's sea cliffs, with which the project is so intimately linked. (*Fig. 03*) The floors were also hand-made, either by laying river cobbles or polishing or stamp molding the cement, which allowed a great deal of freedom of expression to those working on this part of the project. (*Fig. 04*) Doing things by hand implies the use of imperfect tools, using imagination to repair or to improvise, leaving irregular marks on the building and permitting levels of tolerance well above those of contemporary standards of construction. This leads us to two further considerations.

The first is how to incorporate imperfection and a certain degree of uncertainty into construction processes; what Sennett describes as "the intimate, fluid join between problem solving and problem finding."[3] Today imperfection in construction is related to error, and is standardized with the measure of tolerance. The undeclared obsession of the modern movement with precision has created, according to Francesca Hughes, "the architect's increasingly conflicted relations to material tolerance and the inflated value of precision they have erected" and the "fear of error that underpins contemporary architectural culture."[4]

If we no longer oppose the "material intolerance" that error implies and accept the imperfections of work done by hand as an artisanal quality of construction, then we can accept higher levels of tolerance and incorporate the idea of the laboratory into the construction itself. The imperfect tests in this laboratory leave traces—visible in the completed building—as a part of the record of the construction.

Le Corbusier was the first to discover and accept these irregular traces left by the formwork and the workmanship in the construction of the Unité d'Habitation in Marseille, where:

> The careful, perfect assembly of the boards of the formwork, initially intended to even attempt the production of a concrete as similar as possible to the smoothed surface of plaster, leads to the discovery of the unexpected, disconcerting beauty of all the inevitable flaws in workmanship generated by the formwork themselves and by the pouring, in years marked by tight construction budgets imposed by the necessities of postwar reconstruction.[5]

2 Richard Sennett, *The Craftsman*, New Haven: Yale University Press, 2008, p. 27.

3 *Ibid.*, p. 33.

4 Francesca Hughes, *The Architecture of Error*, Cambridge: MIT Press, 2014, p. 3

5 Roberto Gargiani and Anna Rossellini, Le Corbusier: *Béton Brut and Ineffable Space, 1940-1965*, Lausanne: EPFL Press, 2011, p. 54.

Fig. 05. Place of Remembrance, builders' handprints

Fig. 06. Paracas Museum under construction

Fig. 08. University of Piura's lecture halls, west facade latticework

Fig. 07. Moquegua Regional Government's Offices, precast panels

Fig. 09. University of Piura's lecture halls, lattice prefabrication

What happens if these traces are no longer an inevitable defect and become an open possibility of generating meaning in our way of relating to the construction?

As our friend, the Spanish architect Juan Carlos Sancho pointed out to us, by acting in this way, the plans, which are documents that anticipate a future action, lose their primacy and the building "becomes a map"—the record of an action that took place in the past—related to the *act of constructing*. This act of constructing becomes a record of human intervention, the traces of which are visible in the building itself.

In the Place of Remembrance, all these traces were left in place, allowing the map of uncertainties, changes, and errors to be read, together with the care, determination and skill of those who built it with their own hands, which ended up imprinted on the entrance wall, beneath the public plaza. In this way, the building relates to memory not only because of its contents but through its actual construction process. (*Fig. 05*)

For the Paracas Museum we took a decision to employ the technique used to polish pre-Colombian ceramics on the exterior surfaces. With a concrete structure and masonry walls, the building was clad with a pozzolanic cement that was polished by hand with a smooth trowel. The marks of the craftsmen who worked on the façades are visible, together with the repairs and alterations. (*Fig. 06*)

The capacity of buildings to draw maps depends not only on what is made by hand, but also on the tolerance levels we accept in the materials we use. For the Moquegua Regional Government Offices we used pre-fabricated panels that served as single-use formwork for the ring-shaped structure. Two hues of concrete were produced using different aggregates, allowing for a high level of tolerance. The lack of precision in the mixing process led to a wide range of tones, which gives the impression either that the façade is constructed of monumental stones, or that a sophisticated technology has been used to give a different shade to each of the almost 600 panels used. (*Fig. 07*) In Piura, the screen panels were manufactured in situ in order to save money, to the detriment of the tolerances calculated at the outset. In agreement with the clients and the builder, it was decided to place them on the west façade, as planned, while taking into account that they would not all fit on the 70 linear meters of frontage. In the end, a decision was taken to leave large construction joints at two points, (*Figs. 08 and 09*) and the surplus panels were inserted in the ground as support walls for the bicycle park, a few dozen meters from the building.

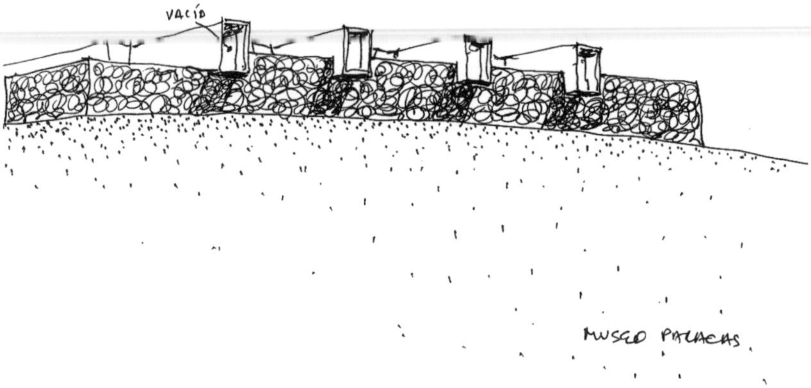
VACÍO
MUSEO PARACAS

Paracas Museum

Location
Paracas National Reserve,
Ica, Peru

Schedule
CONTEST August 2008
PROJECT October 2008 — March 2010
WORK June 2011 — May 2012
OPENING July 2016

Floor Area
1,220 m^2

Client
Spanish Agency for International Development Cooperation (AECID)
Ministry of Culture

Project Manager
Rodrigo Apolaya

Structural Engineering
Antonio Blanco

Construction
Consorcio Paracas

In 2008, the European Union, through the Spanish International Development Agency (AEICD) organized a competition to rebuild the site museum for the Paracas culture (700 BCE-200 CE). Originally built in 1964, it was destroyed by the devastating 2007 earthquake. Our proposal started by considering this act of reconstruction as a layer to be added to the thousands accumulated or deposited by both human and natural actions. For us, the project should both alter the landscape and depend on it at the same time, just as a stone or a mark in the desert would. Part of these layers on the landscape are pre-existing: the adjacent interpretation center and record of the original museum, demolished and dismantled after the earthquake, thus preserving its memory was our first intention. We decided to maintain the same footprint, not only to continue the cultural construction but to avoid occupying new areas of the desert, given the archeological excavations that this would necessarily entail.

The building also maintains the prismatic geometry of its predecessor, with a volumetry that reinforces its subtle presence in the desert, inserting itself into an ancient cultural landscape. The construction's mass and red hue enable it to merge more easily with the sacred hills that hold the burial sites, which are red, ferrous stone. We decided to approach the budget limitations as an opportunity rather than an obstacle. Since the budget only covered a painted render finish, we again turned to the technique used to polish pre-Colombian pottery: red pozzolanic cement, a material that is resistant to the efflorescence caused by the salts of the arid soil. We had discovered this technique building our houses, and in applying it to a project on this scale we showed that hand-polished cement costs no more than a painted finish.

The marks left by the builders as they polish the cement confers on the museum an appearance reminiscent of ceramics, evoking the finish of the pre-Colombian pieces on display inside. Due to its iron content, the cement tends to change its appearance over time, becoming darker and acquiring a patina that is not due to wear but rather to the harmless oxidation of the cement. As a result the museum not only bears witness to our ancestral cultures, but is also itself a time-sensitive map inserted in an ancient landscape.

Inside, the exhibition galleries' structure is an apparently contradictory hybrid between the labyrinthine spaces and the spiral routes of the ancient Peruvians, and the fluid and transparent spatiality of contemporary architecture. The environmental demands of the desert and the exhibition design demands of the collection are resolved thanks to an environmental correction mechanism that defines the architectural and exhibition design parti pris. This mechanism comprises a continuous skylight beneath which are located the transition spaces between exhibition galleries or circulation spaces, according to requirements and their position in the project. This mechanism regulates the natural and artificial lighting, natural ventilation, and potential future cooling of the rooms. Its geometry reinterprets the characteristic offset of Paracas ancient textiles, their most notable technological and artistic form of expression.

MUSEO DE SITIO
JULIO C. TELLO

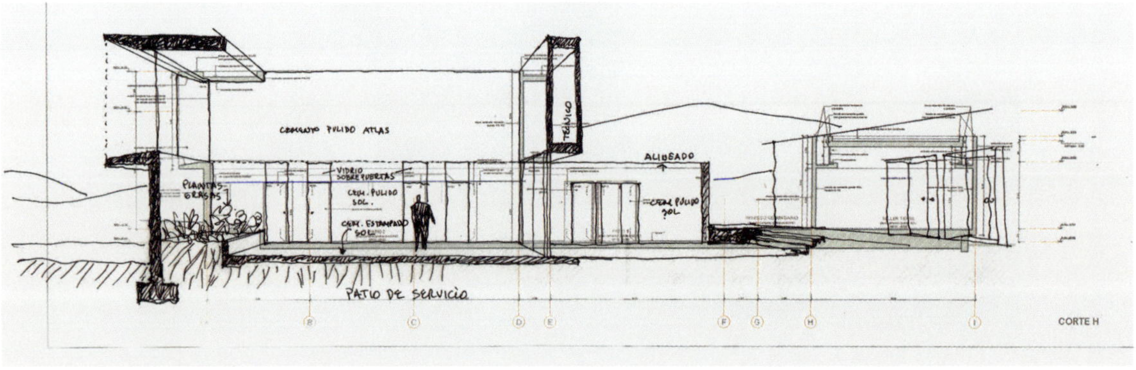
CEMENTO PULIDO ATLAS
TÉCNICO
ALIGERADO
VIDRIO SOBRE PUERTAS
PLANTAS GRASAS
CEM. PULIDO SOL.
CEM. ESTAMPADO SOL
CEM. PULIDO SOL
PATIO DE SERVICIO
B
C
D
E
F
G
H
I
CORTE H

Upper floor plan
Ground floor plan
Section

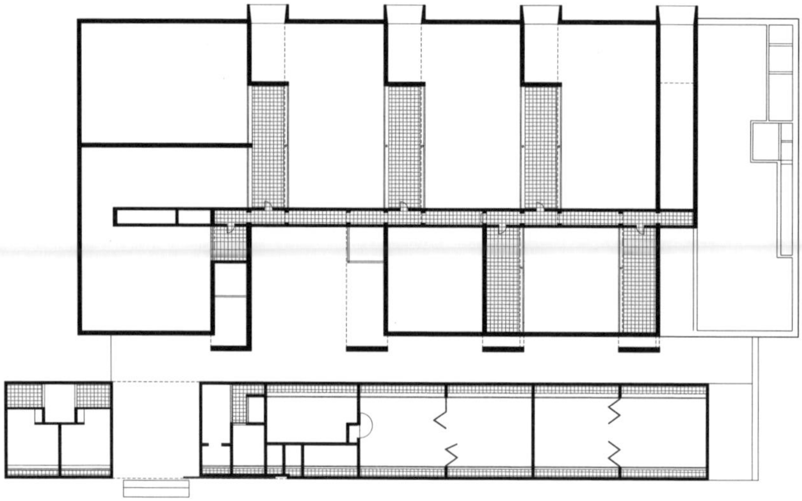

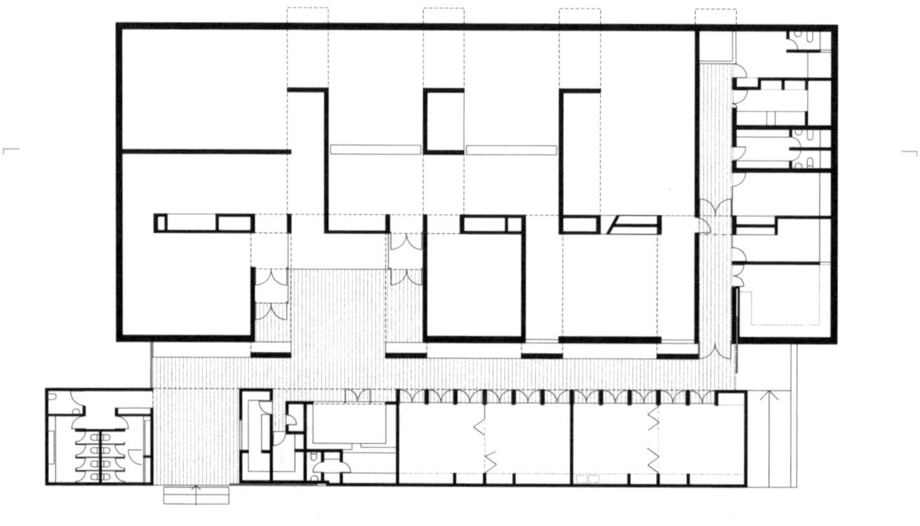

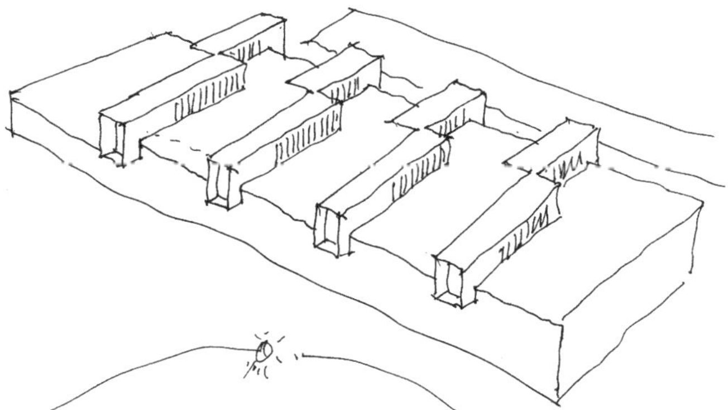

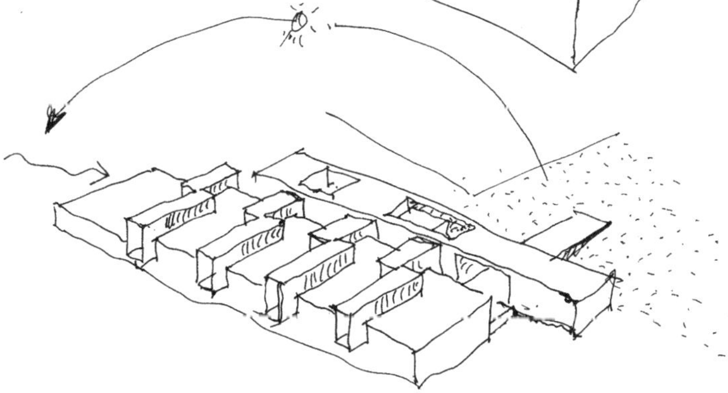

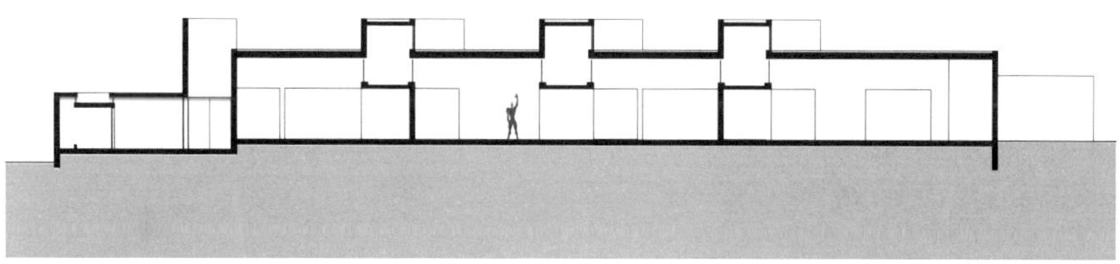

jedores del desierto
Desert weavers

Pioneros de la arqueología en Paracas

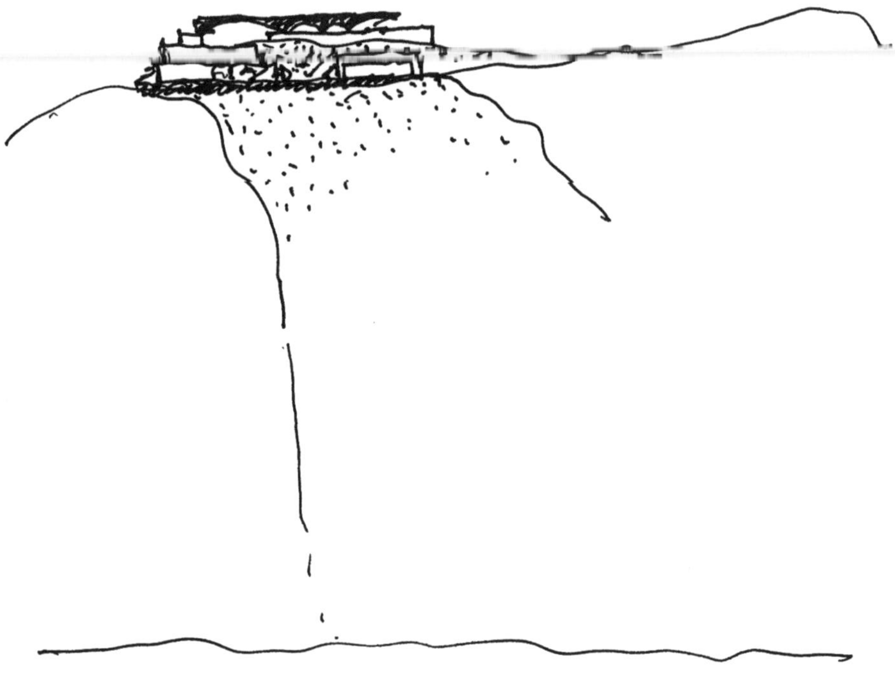

C3 House

Location
Ancón, Lima, Peru

Schedule
PROJECT 2013 — 2014
WORK 2014 — 2016

Lot Area
1,830 m²

Floor Area
547 m²

Design Team
Eduardo Zambrano
Blecker Ruiz

Structural Engineering
Jorge Indacochea

Construction
Rubén Cavallini

This project is located at the confluence of two abstract surfaces: the horizontal expanse of the Pacific Ocean, and the rough, undulating surface of the desert. The site is to the north of Lima, in an extremely arid territory where the temperature range almost perfectly matches the human comfort zone. It seems to be an incomplete landscape, always unfinished and undefined, yet remaining benign to human beings.

Despite the house's large size, simple and very low-tech construction processes—made possible by the benevolent climate—allowed a small team of builders under the leadership of master builder Rubén Cavallini to construct it. Even though this lengthened the construction time to two years, it also opened up the process to experimentation, and trial and error. The house is sited on a plot containing large boulders that were left in place, determining a parti pris broken down into four volumes. The smaller rocks were removed, shaped, and used as part of the construction. The remainder was finished with the polished cement technique—as used for the Paracas Museum—to mimic the material and color of the sea cliffs. Great effort went into constructing the concrete vaults, made with traditional formwork and stuccoed interior walls.

As in earlier houses, the platform was proposed as a strategy to create a habitable space in the desert: a horizontal surface inserted in the sloping topography and defining the living area both in terms of its space—which opens up to the sky and horizon alike—and in the space it leaves between it and the natural land surface. The absence of rain and the mild temperatures in both summer and winter permit the program to expand across the site without compromising the comfort of occupants. Three platforms were created on the rough, steeply sloping ground to offer a wide variety of living spaces, sheltered by a green roof in the more private areas and concrete vaults in the social spaces. In the latter, the vaults help "anchor" the space to the ground. Visible from afar, the roof appears as incomplete as the landscape that it echoes: a hidden vault, a visible vault, and a vault that extends outward without finding a support to provide balance.

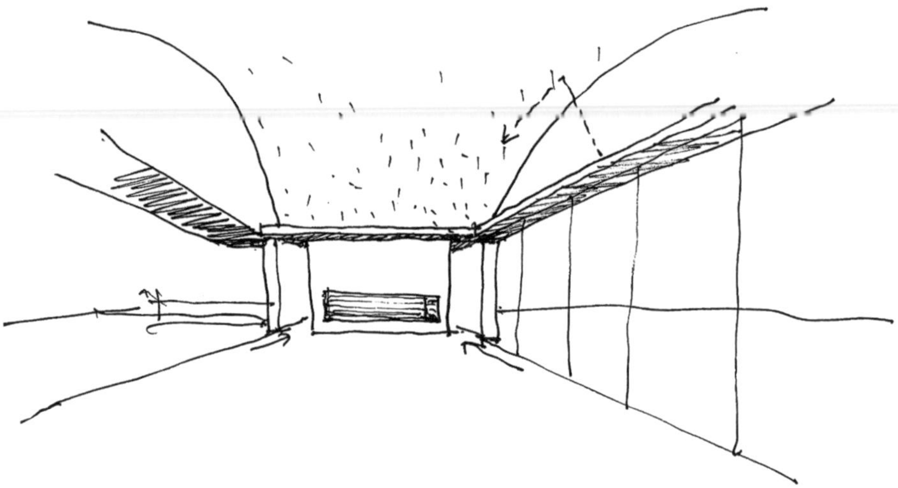

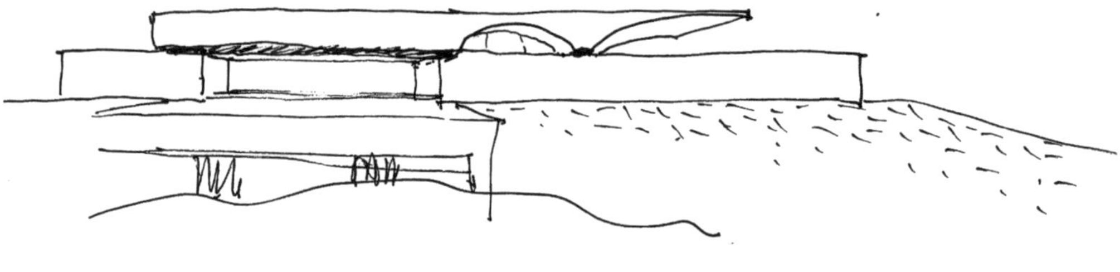

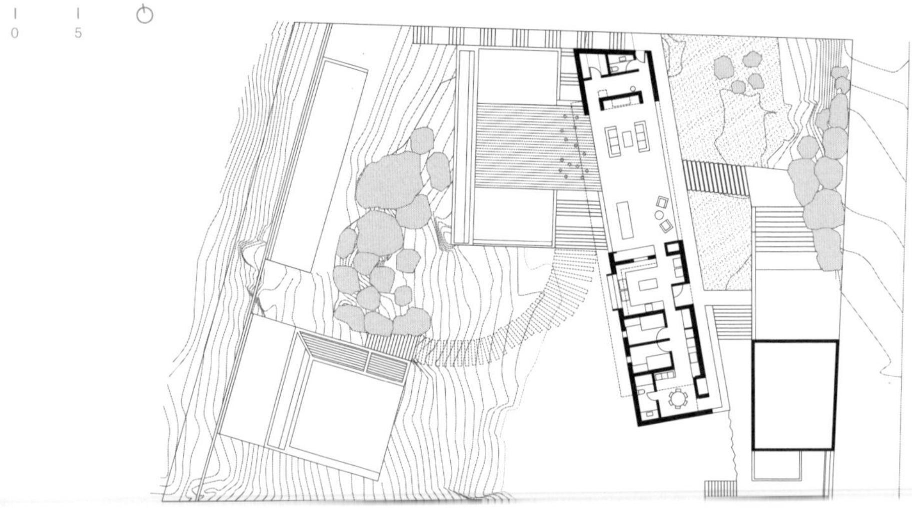
0
5

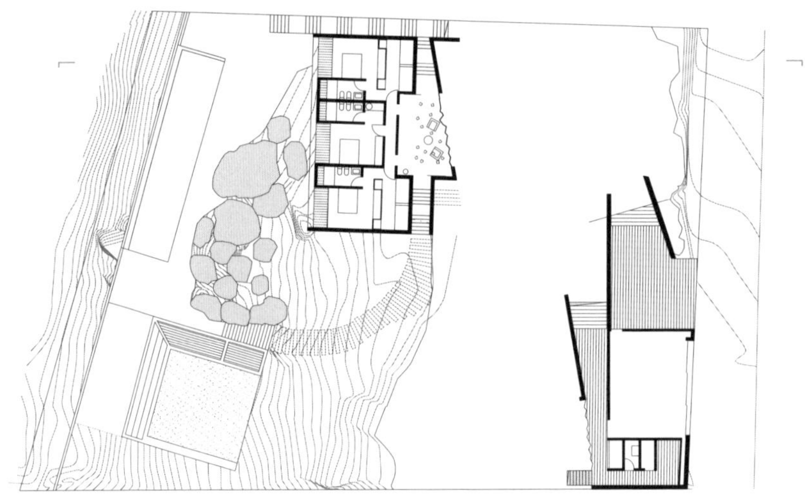

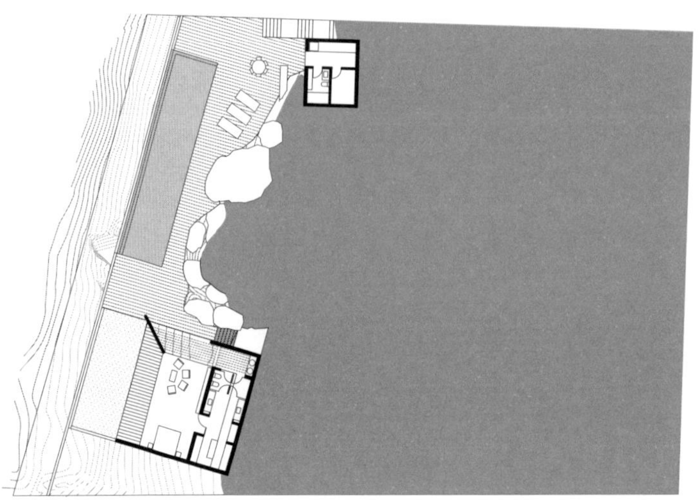

Level 1 floor plan
Ground floor plan
Level -1 floor plan

Axonometric
Section

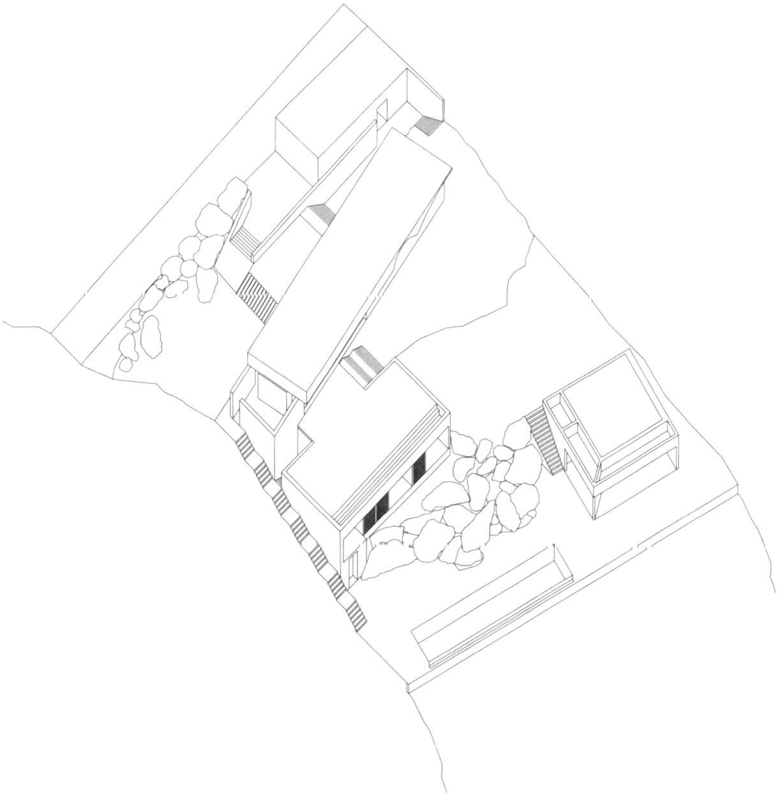

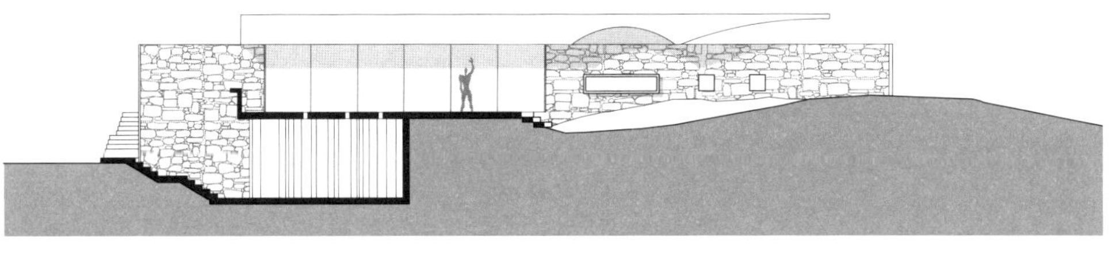

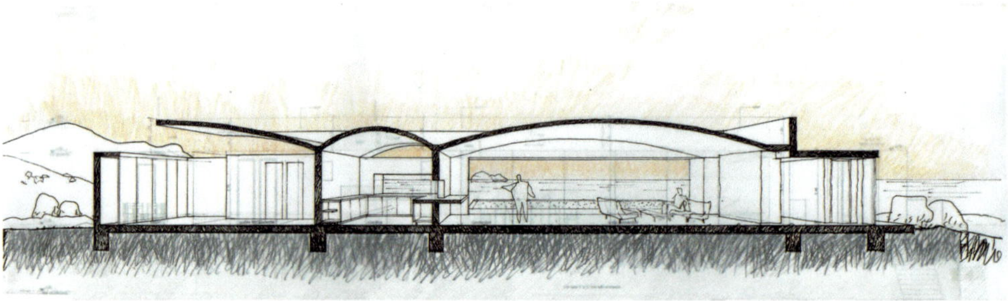

Fig. 04. Victor Hugo Building, Montreuil

Fig. 03. Farnsworth House, visit photograph

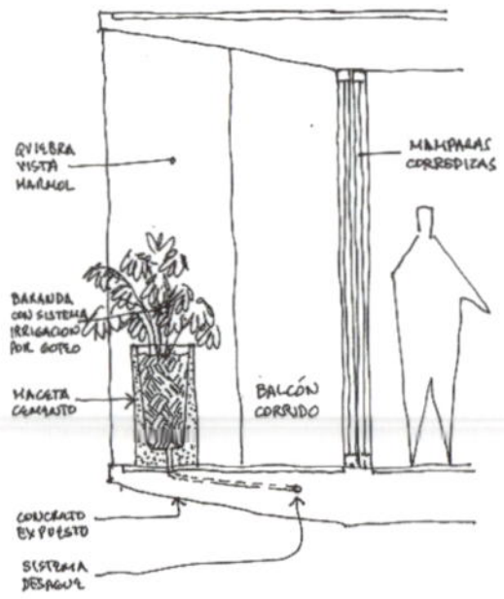

Fig. 09. NU Building, sketch

Fig. 06. DUO Building, render

Fig. 05. Junín Building

Fig. 10. SB Building

Fig. 01. Colonial balcony

Fig. 02. *Tapada limeña*

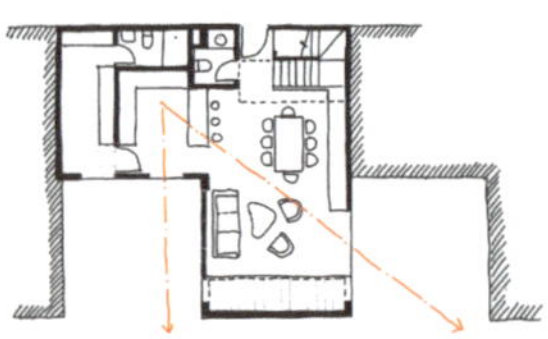

Fig. 08. MG Building

Fig. 07. MG Building

The Thickness of Intimacy

The deepening of intimacy has been a constant area of interest in our approach to living spaces. While for private houses the enclosure and the platform have proven effective in creating intimacy within the immensity of the desert, this holds much less true for collective housing. In urban settings, the search for intimacy makes more sense in its relation to the lifestyle of a building's occupants than in its connection to the landscape.

The Moorish legacy in Lima's society has resulted in a significant introversion in how people lived in the past and today; therefore, it also influences the relationship between people's dwellings and the city. The idea of "seeing and not being seen" during the viceregal period and the early days of the post-independence Peru had a broad influence, from people's attire to urban façades. The roots of this notion are more evident in North Africa than in Spain: the *tapada limeña*—the veiled woman of Lima—referred to the type of dress women used in public, covering themselves with a veil or shawl that left just one eye uncovered. Meanwhile the famed balconies of Lima are prisms defined by a lattice appended to the opaque façades of the house, which allowed the city to be observed from the intimacy of the home without being seen from the street. (*Figs. 01 and 02*)

Although Ebenezer Howard's paradigm of the Garden City had spread around the world in the early 20th century, in Lima this new way of conceiving the city was limited to the laying out of curved, tree-lined streets in new developments, and never extended to larger lots or detached houses surrounded by gardens. Instead, the tendency was to close houses off from the outside world by turning living spaces inward, defined sometimes by courtyards and most frequently by perimeter walls.

Leaving aside the particularities of Lima's citizens, intimacy is an essential aspect of dwelling. In *The Poetics of Space,* Gaston Bachelard refers to the "power of attraction of all the domains of intimacy. There does not exist a real intimacy that is repellent. All the spaces of intimacy are designated by an abstraction. Their being is well-being."[1]

We consider it impossible to think about housing without thinking about intimacy. Even in the most extreme case, Farnsworth House, the total transparency towards the exterior did not entail a loss of intimacy, insofar as this is protected by the surrounding woodland. The private space was not delimited by the glazed surfaces but by the forest clearing around it and the large tree—now gone—on its south side. (*Fig. 03*) Years later, when the bridge was built across the river—just a few dozen meters away—and hundreds of visitors arrived, drawn by the fame of the house, the forest clearing lost its ability to secure that sense of intimacy: at that moment the house became uninhabitable.

Nor is the notion of immensity only a physical concept, as we consider it in the relationship between habitat and desert landscape. Immensity can also exist in, and be created by, intimate surroundings. Bachelard says that "concerning this immensity, Baudelaire has just told us in detail, that it is a conquest of intimacy. Grandeur progresses in the world in proportion to the deepening of intimacy."[2]

Sandra Barclay
Jean Pierre Crousse

1 Gaston Bachelard, *The Poetics of Space*, New York: Penguin, 2014 [1958], p. 34.

2 *Ibid.*, p. 212.

In our multi-family housing projects we have explored how immensity emerges in the deepening of intimacy. Stacking housing units reveals that the relationship between the intimacy of the indoors and the public nature of the outdoors is achieved on the horizontal plane, and is piled up vertically. The thickness created between these two spaces makes it possible to generate the necessary threshold to give depth to intimacy.

Japan is one country that has developed a particularly sophisticated culture of transitions. In Japanese, the term *ma* means interval, space, duration, and in traditional painting and architecture represents the void that lends meaning to the elements it separates. The word *en* means relationship or connection, and gives rise to the *engawa* or space in which the concepts of interior and exterior are blurred. Our first journey to Japan, in 2012, and Augustin Berque's writings, opened our minds to the possibility that a multi-family apartment building can be a vertical *engawa*, mediating between the public exterior and the private interior, as a space dependent on both yet capable of modifying them as well. In his *Le sens de l'space au Japon*, Berque emphasizes that "the Japanese preference for intermediate zones over vertical separations is expressed in two ways. Firstly, the intermediate space constitutes a clear and obligatory passage to soften the contrast between the two other spaces of the interior and exterior." He defines *genkan* as "where you are already in the building, but not yet in the home," and the *engawa* as "where you are neither inside nor outside."[3]

When we completed our first housing project, in Montreuil, Paris, we had already accumulated extensive experience in designing collective habitats, developed over the years Sandra spent studying with Henri Ciriani, while Jean Pierre worked in his studio on social housing projects. The limitations of this type of housing did not stop us from creating in Montreuil thicknesses in the social areas of the apartments, taking advantage of the displacements in the linear building, as anticipated in the Montreuil urban plan developed by Álvaro Siza, Christian Devillers, Michel Corajoud, and Laurent Beaudouin, which helped open up views towards the city center. (*Fig. 04*) However, this thickness did not yet constitute a true vertical *engawa*.

Many years later, we designed a small building in the historical district of Barranco, formerly a seaside resort for Lima residents and now incorporated into the city. The regulations for listed buildings required a façade aligned along the street and a maximum lot coverage of 30%. This encouraged us to work our hardest to create depth. Without enough surface area for an underground parking garage, we allocated the open space between the façade on the street and the building, which was set back six meters, to a ground-floor parking area. Above this area, the thickness was exploited to create large, offset balconies for each apartment, establishing an intermediate space for encounters between neighbors, similar to the succession of pools in the Vedoble houses. In this building, the shift is from the intimacy of the apartment to a collective area for neighbors in the intermediate space, which in turn relates to the urban space via the façade on

3 Augustin Berque and Maurice Sauzet, *Le sens de l'espace au Japon*, Paris: Arguments, 2004, p. 90.

the street. The building regulations also insisted on vertical window openings, so a sequence was created to make up a mosaic of transparencies towards the city, which appears as if "edited" in a series of frames. The intermediate space is the site of this immensity in intimacy, and in turn produces an indoor-exterior space. (*Fig. 05*)

Another project that explores the immensity of intermediate space was one we worked on with our friend the architect Jaime Rouillon in San José, Costa Rica. The DUO building is located in the former National Botanic Garden, now the Simón Bolívar Park, close to the city center. Our design was to verticalize tropical vegetation, with a concrete structure that houses tree-filled garden terraces in double- and quadruple-height spaces. The structure links to another one that contains the duplex apartments, but the intermediate space is almost as large as the interior of these apartments. In this case, the depth and exuberance of the vegetation merges with the backdrop of the park. It gives the impression of living in a house in the forest. (*Fig. 06*)

In the MG building, the loggias open up laterally towards courtyards that generate depth between the space of the street and the space of intimacy, producing diagonal views and preserving a distance between neighbors in the relatively narrow street. (*Figs. 07 and 08*)

The NU building seeks to achieve this same depth without physically having it. To paraphrase Colin Rowe and Robert Slutzky[4], we could speak of a phenomenal depth determined by the inherent qualities of the organization of planes and spaces. A series of view-breaks, triangular in plan, are aligned along the length of a subtly curved façade, generating depth by its geometry and the presence of cylindrical planters that function as parapets. The bedrooms of each floor's two apartments are located along this east-facing façade. The view-breaks operate not only from the inside looking out, but also vice-versa. The façade's thickness, as part of the shared property, preserves the unitary character of the building over time, irrespective of any future changes to the apartments' layout. (*Fig. 09*)

The 200 housing-unit complex recently completed in San Bartolo also plays with phenomenal depth. The narrow site sets two linear buildings facing each other across a shared garden. To avoid direct overlooks, the apartments are offset in plan view, producing diagonal vistas over the garden. The loggias acquire geometries that vary according to the routes taken by apartment owners through the garden, protecting the intimacy of the residents. (*Fig. 10*)

4 Colin Rowe and Robert Slutsky, *Transparency*, Basilea: Birkhäuser, 1997.

NU Building

Location
Miraflores, Lima, Peru

Schedule
PROJECT August 2014 — May 2015
WORK October 2015 — March 2017

Lot Area
800 m²

Floor Area
8,125 m²

Promoter
Quatro Inmobiliaria

Project Manager
María Isabel Pineda

Structural Engineering
Luis Flores

Construction
EF Contratistas

The project responds to the privileged situation of an urban lot with three sides, proposing an eight-story building that is sensitive to its outlooks and the characteristics of the surrounding urban spaces. To this end we calibrated the openings in relation to the views, orientations, and sound levels of the adjacent urban spaces.

The project articulates the relationship between an enclosed park, to the south of the building, a cul-de-sac to the east, and the public thoroughfare to the north. We created differentiated transition spaces that make it possible to generate the necessary depth to intensify the sensation of intimacy. The building opens up towards the park, while sheltering from the views and noise of the cul-de-sac and public road. The treatment of these three different façades is expressed in a succession of ribbon balconies that narrow on their outer edge, giving the impression of a stack of transitional spaces, rather than of housing units.

The longest façade is east-facing, overlooking the cul-de-sac, where a public parking lot and the pedestrian entrance to the building are located. The ribbon balconies curve gently to indicate their character as the principal façade. The building is protected with panels of local marble, which function as louvers to protect both from the sun and from views from the outside, sheltering the bedrooms from the morning sun and from overlooks from adjacent buildings. These elements are interspersed with vegetation planted in cylindrical tubs, with a drip-fed irrigation system integrated into the railings. Our proposal was for this thickness to be a collective property and responsibility, shared by all owners, which would require a minimum level of agreement—such as the choice of plants—while meaning the way the building expresses itself outwardly is an ongoing joint agreement and not just imposed by the architecture.

In plan view, the design aligns the bedrooms along the east-facing façade, allowing for variation in the apartment typology—a feature often sought when it comes to selling a commercial building. With the bedrooms of the two apartments per floor arranged along this "collective thickness" of the louvers and planters, a certain homogenous character can be maintained despite potential interior variations.

Initially designed with two units per floor (three and four bedrooms) the building acquired greater diversity during the process of sale and construction, even including on one floor a single apartment with three façades.

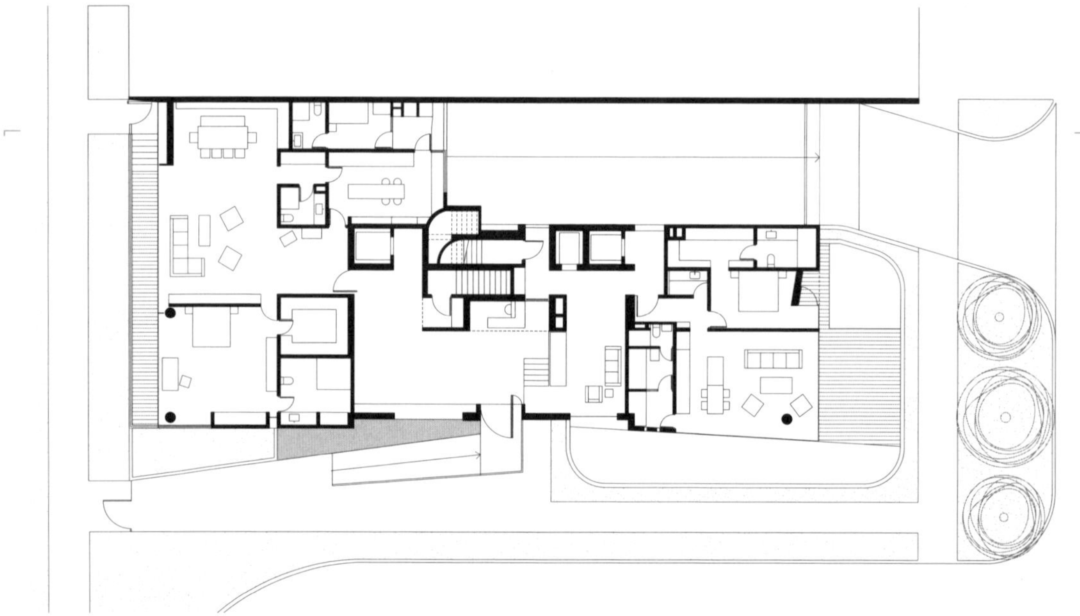

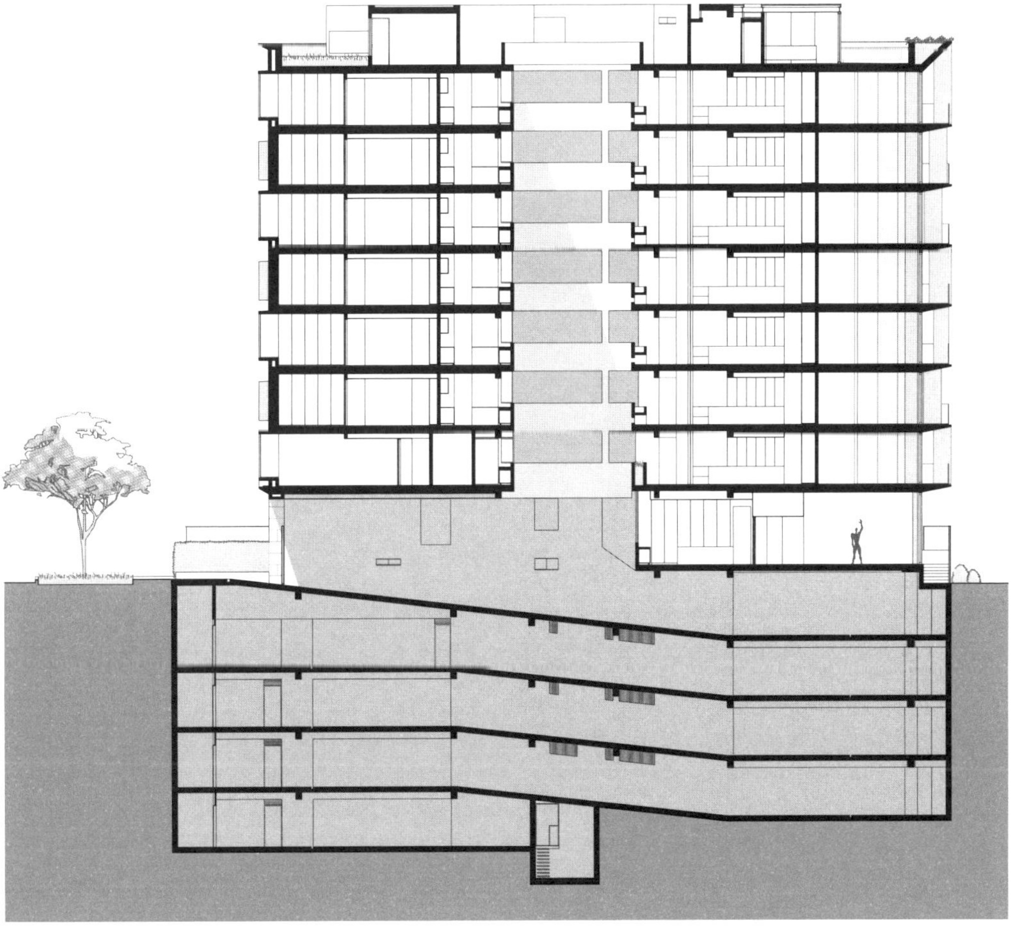

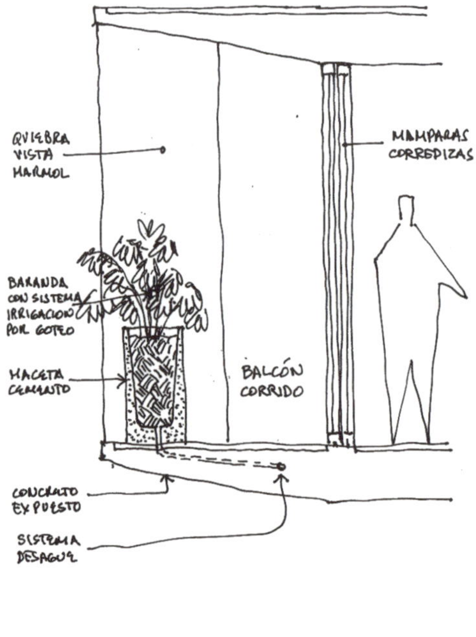
QUIEBRA
VISTA
MARMOL
MAMPARAS
CORREDIZAS
BARANDA
CON SISTEMA
IRRIGACION
POR GOTEO
MACETA
CEMENTO
BALCÓN
CORRIDO
CONCRETO
EXPUESTO
SISTEMA
DESAGUE

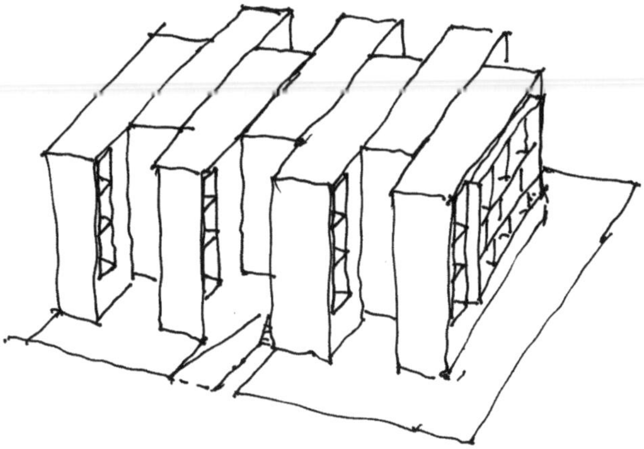

MG Building

Location
Surco, Lima, Peru

Schedule
PROJECT January 2012 — May 2013
WORK June 2013 — December 2017

Lot Area
960 m²

Floor Area
3,140 m²

Promoter
Edward Barclay

Design Team
Alejandro Zamudio
Paulo Shimabukuro

Structural Engineering
Raúl Ríos

Construction
Modutec SAC

Artwork (lobby)
Daniel Barclay

This project is inserted into a fairly dense, homogenous district of five-story buildings with dividing walls between them and relatively narrow streets. The program required a high level of diversity in the type of apartments, which varied between 100 and 500 m². We decided to locate the larger apartments on the ground floor, offering the possibility of having a private garden, and on the top floor, with two-story "houses" with a green roof. Occupying the intermediate levels are seven duplex L-shaped apartments with spatial expansions resulting from a diagonal treatment of the space.

The structure is organized into six-meter-wide strips, perpendicular to the longest, street-facing façade. These are displaced in plan to generate the folding of the exterior perimeter, increasing the external surface—like the fins of a radiator—and providing natural light to all spaces.

The volumetric displacement creates interior and exterior courtyards with one side open onto the street, allowing a number of the existing trees to be retained and generating intimacy in a relatively tight urban space overlooked by adjacent buildings. These courtyards are glazed and framed by opaque vertical elements in reinforced concrete. In this building, the displacement of the structure and the folding of the façade are the elements that define the depth of the intermediate space between the private and the public domains. Behind the vertical elements we installed a number of double-height terraces, generating supplementary depth, and forming—like the pools in the Vedoble houses—the privileged space of encounters among neighbors.

The program is arranged to make room for a semi-basement parking garage, intersected by the two rear courtyards, helping to introduce natural light. This enabled two trees to be planted, integrating it with the rest of the building. On the ground floor, the entrance lobby defines a covered, indoor-exterior space communicating with several floors via an integrated staircase, while providing direct entry to two apartments. On the second floor there are seven duplex apartments and, on the fourth floor, two duplex apartments with roof gardens.

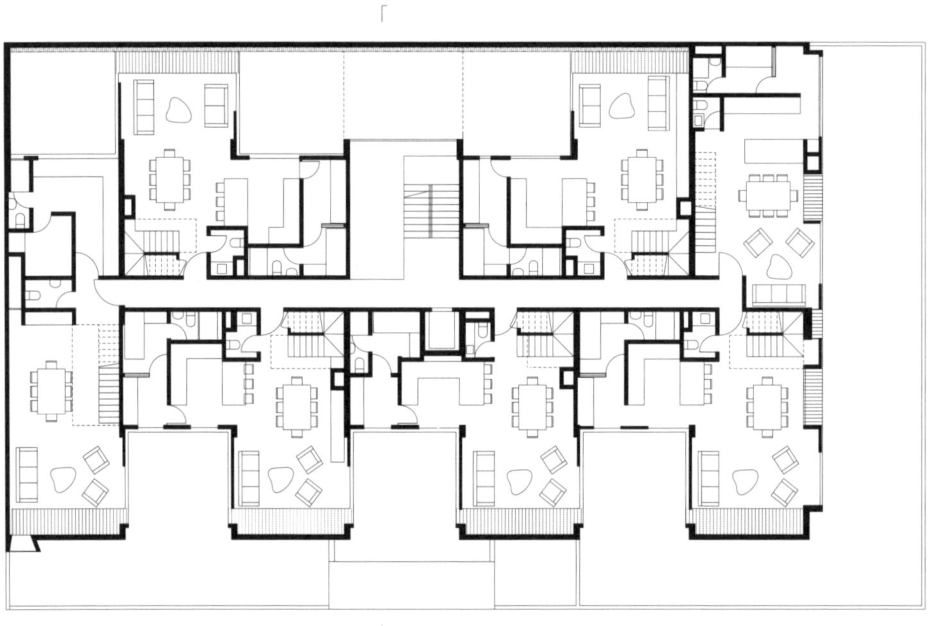

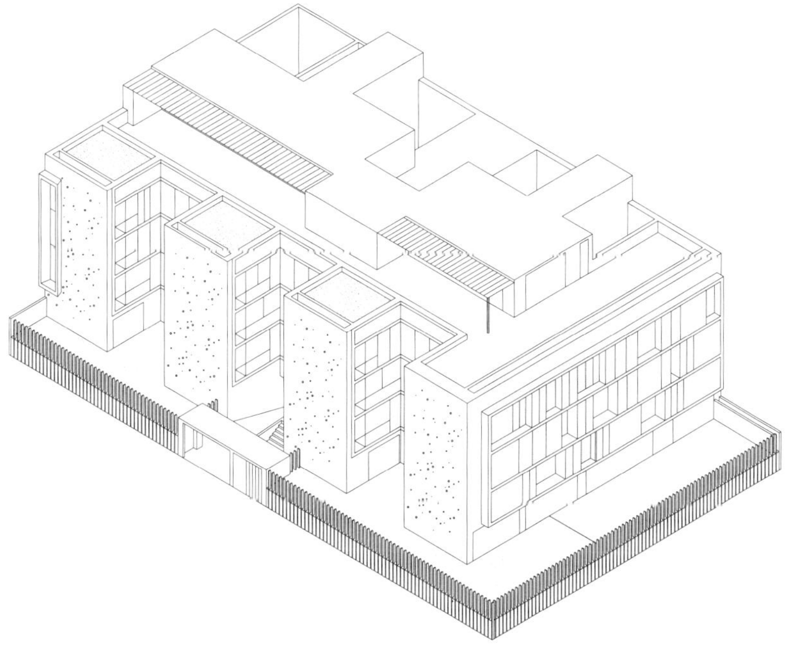

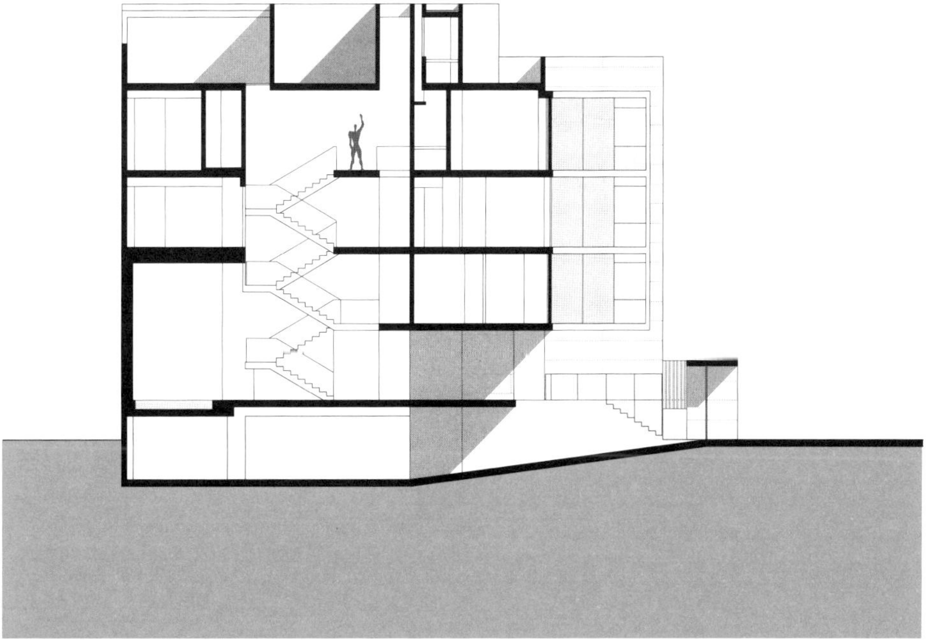

DUPLEX A

III

Learning Landscapes

Edificio E
Mies Crown Hall
Americas Prize
2018 Winner

Statement by the Jury

The University of Piura's Edificio E is an architectural work of extraordinary intelligence and sensitivity. Set in a dry forest almost 1,000 kilometers northwest of Lima, the building accommodates a growing student population, the result of a public grant promoting enrollment by disadvantaged rural students. The building is made up of a series of lecture halls and administrative offices arranged into a square; these 11 small structures are woven together by a network of interstitial, semi-exterior pathways and public spaces, creating informal areas for students to pause and interact with one another. Sandra Barclay and Jean Pierre Crousse describe the building as a "learning landscape," a shaded, airy environment that encourages students to exchange ideas.

The deceptive simplicity and modesty of Edificio E conceals and reveals a building of unexpected complexity, intensity and richness. Responding to the harshness of the sun and extreme dry heat of the savannah landscape of northern Peru, the design defines a dense, inner world of unexpected softness and openness shrouded by porous concrete screens.

Like a vernacular village of narrow streets and open spaces—so typical of organic urban models across Latin America—the building compresses the collective human experience. A sequence of interconnected ramps, corridors, balconies and open spaces are hewn out of the orthogonal concrete mass, like crevices and ravines formed in mountain ranges over geological time. For Barclay & Crousse, the three-dimensional, sectional experience dominates the dynamics of habitation and occupation.

Jury Chair Ricky Burdett notes that Edificio E sets a new compact model for the 21st-century university building that celebrates cohesiveness and economy of expression. "By reducing its footprint and optimizing its shading potential, the building is more resource-efficient, less land-hungry and maximizes passive environmental control. At the same time, its very compactness forces its users to come together, optimizing the democratic potential of a building inhabited by young people for generations to come."

Jury member Rodrigo Pérez de Arce similarly notes how Edificio E's inventive yet economical approach works at a typological level. "It is not just a project but an exploration of a type, and therefore a set of spatial notions that invites emulation and even replication," he says. "The building is technically undemanding for its simple rules and its recourse to well-tried materials and well-established building procedures."

The jury also remarked on Edificio E's thoughtful attention to its site, especially its demanding climate and risk of earthquakes. "This is perhaps the first building I have seen where the trees were as important as the classrooms," says jury member Claire Weisz. "And it's inspiring to see the idea of designing for earthquakes resulting in a building that is at the same time many buildings, with a shared roof that both ties them together and is still open enough to create a village of individual elements."

In drawing a connection between Edificio E and Crown Hall, Denison says, "Mies's Crown Hall represents a fundamental enrichment in the understanding of how architects enclose and define

space. I believe Edificio E will become a similar point of reference, but here it is the space between that enriches the collective architectural language."

To realize Edificio E, Barclay & Crousse worked closely with the commissioning client, María Pía Chirinos, Research Vice-Provost of the University of Piura. "The trust, respect and friendship between us was essential for us to fully grasp the aspirations of the university and for the clients to accept an innovative building type that was inspired by their aspirations, the act of learning and the campus landscape," Barclay & Crousse say.

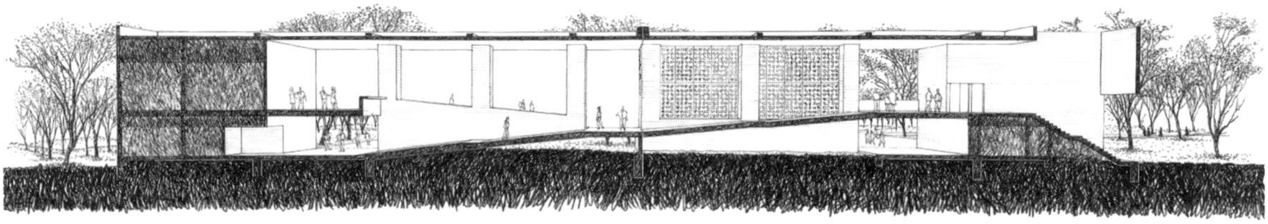

Edificio E University of Piura

Location
Piura, Peru

Schedule
PROJECT December 2014 — May 2015
WORK June 2015 — March 2016

Floor Area
9,400 m²

Project Manager
David Leininger

Structural Engineering
Higashi Ingenieros

Construction
Huarcaya Construcción — Ingeniería

The University of Piura has a 130-hectare campus amid a dry forest landscape, typical of north Peru's desert region, and now surrounded by the city of Piura. A growing student population of limited financial means have been able to enrol at the university thanks to the government's Beca 18 grant program, requiring an additional university campus building for lecture halls, workshops and offices for faculty members from different departments.

We set out to create a learning atmosphere rather than an architectonic type or shape; we decided on this new approach because we considered that the "pavilion" layout was no longer appropriate for new learning landscapes. The idea is based on two main ideas: firstly, a space was needed to accommodate new kinds of learning through casual encounters and the possibility of studying and exchanging knowledge outside the formal classroom environment. Secondly, the spaces needed to be comfortable in Piura's predominantly hot, sunny and dry climate, cooled by light southerly breezes.

Students can find refuge in the new spaces just as the compact city is sheltered from the vastness of the desert, and just as the campus, a desert void, is protected from the city: creating a familiar yet unexpected environment. Emulating how the apparently leafy foliage of the dry forest covers a desert land of sand and shade, the lecture hall hides a surprising inner world.

Seen from the exterior, the construction appears compact and geometrically pure (70 x 70m), oriented according to the cardinal points. The interior reveals a set of 11 independent, two- and three-story buildings, beneath a generous roof that provides shade for the many different communal spaces and passages. The separation between these various buildings ensures good cross-ventilation and natural lighting for the exterior and interior spaces. The building's various roofs are barely separated, with louvers allowing light to filter through but preventing direct sunlight hitting the upper parts of the interiors.

The buildings' layout creates a rational, square circulation area and also produces labyrinthine interstitial spaces between the blocks. Five types of construction create a world to be discovered along several routes, connected by ramps and stairs, and punctuated by places to sit, small cafés, dry gardens and terrace seating.

The building is inserted into a clearing in the forest, and although compact it is still accessible through various entrances to the campus. Its outer appearance is defined by the orientation of its sides: the northern and southern façades use vertical brise soleils that help regulate solar gain in this intertropical region, while the east and west facing aspects have louvers that filter the sunlight, as well as intermediate outer spaces that prevent heat from entering by conduction into the interiors.

0 15

A-A Section B-B Section
Ground floor plan Level 1 floor plan

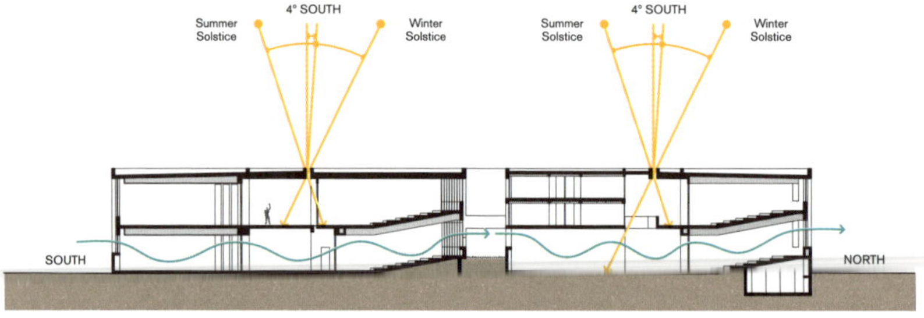

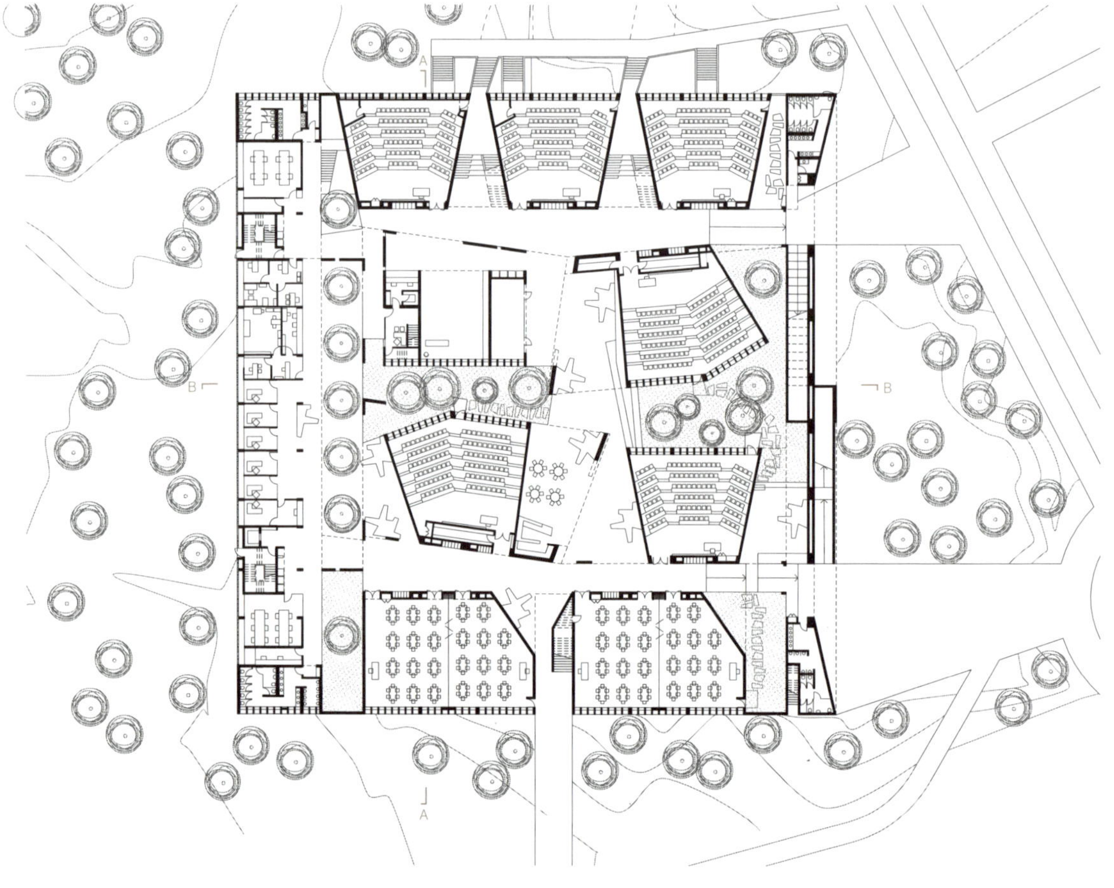

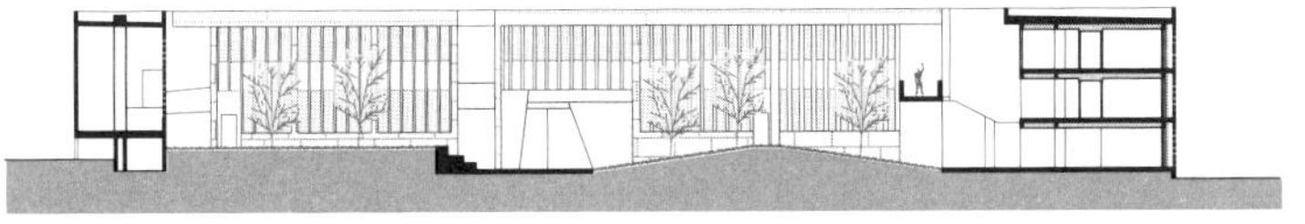

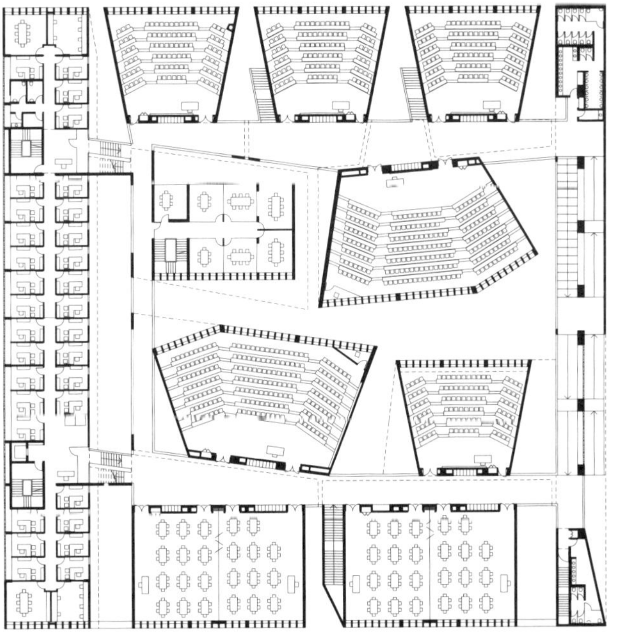

Chasing the Shadows

Sandra Barclay's and Jean Pierre Crousse's Edificio E, a university campus building in northern Peru, is the winner of the 2018 Mies Crown Hall Americas Prize (MCHAP). The jury recognized Edificio E for its exceptional response to both program and context: the architects re-imagine the social possibilities of warm-climate building typologies to create supportive, dynamic social spaces—and exceptionally beautiful architecture.

Here IIT College of Architecture Dean Reed Kroloff engages Barclay & Crousse in a conversation about the project that elucidates its core architectural strategies and their underlying social agenda.

How did the program for this university building come about?

The program was born thanks to the new "Beca 18" governmental scholarship program, designed to open the doors for public school students of modest rural origins to attend private universities. By accepting 700 of these students, the University of Piura also qualified for a loan that enabled it to increase its educational infrastructure by 30%—which included Edificio E.

Who are the building's users?

The users are students from different origins and backgrounds, as well as faculty from all of the different schools of the university. When you are doing a generic building, it's difficult to determine what its character might be. In this case, we were bringing together economically privileged and underprivileged students, and this was very important to us. This also linked into the landscape and where we were building.

Tell us about working with this client.

The University of Piura had initially retained us for a different project, a campus learning center. So we were already familiar with the site and the client. Then, in the middle of the design process for the learning center, they asked us if we could do Edificio E—in only 15 months. So we had this huge challenge of designing the project, doing the drawings, putting it out to bid, and then building it—all in just over one year. All of the decisions we made during design were based on the fact that we were going to have to build the project only eight months later. The client, the University of Piura, already knew and trusted us, and therefore was ready to listen. They wanted to make sure the building was very high quality, and they were open to new ideas. The building program was already determined by the time we started; what we discussed with them were the possible relations between its various parts. For example, we needed to design a large number of faculty offices. We had long discussions about whether the offices should be open to the students or separate (so the faculty could get their research done). We decided to give the offices privacy, but in order to get to them, the faculty has to cross the entire building and in that way interact with students as much as possible.

Interview with Reed Kroloff

Its exceptional for a Peruvian client to ask for a high-quality project. They usually want it either cheap or iconic, or, worse still, both. That was not the case here. Other people have begun to ask how we achieved such quality, which is beginning to help change the nature of architecture here. It's important that this exceptional building is in Piura, not Lima (where everything in the country happens already). No one can believe it's in this little city. This has been very important for the people there, and the rest of the country as well.

How did the landscape affect your design?

Most of the time, the climate there is very dry. But when El Niño comes—about every 10 or 12 years, tropical rains arrive for four to six months. So after the first El Niño arrived a few years after the creation of the University, they planted many, many trees. They decided to build a forest, rather than buildings. The tree cover lowers the temperature, and the University's planners left gaps within the planting for new buildings. We structured the Edificio E the same way; creating a compound of buildings with gaps between them. The in-between spaces are very important, as places where both student populations can meet. The building works with the same logic as the forest.

Seen from the air, Edificio E almost recalls the plan of an ancient souk. What was your intention in creating such a dense, urban weave?

The intention of the building was to extend the logic of the forest. All the trees were planted in a grid. We built from there. And though we didn't start out trying to do it, we created a little town, a swatch of urban fabric.

The other logic of the forest was that you always move around in the shade (to avoid the sun and heat); we are very near to the equator, so the sun is always vertical. People are always chasing the shadows, walking from tree to tree. We were thinking of exactly this when we were designing the building. Shade was essential. Today, the building is essential on the campus; it is a new center offering shaded spaces ventilated by breezes. Thermal sensation there are four degrees lower than on the rest of the campus. Now, nearly 30% of the people using the building don't even have classes there; they're seeking the shade.

You've described Edificio E as a labyrinth. How do people move through it?

In a labyrinth, you don't fully see where you're going. It slows you down. You have to weave your way through it, so time slows down. It's not a corridor. This is especially true on the ground floor, which has multiple entries. The building is oriented according to the cardinal points. This is for two reasons. Firstly, the earlier buildings on campus were oriented that way. Secondly, because we're so close to the equator, the sun is high above us; we have to protect people from it, especially on the east and west orientations. There is a regular breeze because we are close to the ocean, so the building is permeable, and breezes sweep through it from the south. The wind even accelerates because of a Venturi effect in the building.

How did your design process begin for this building? In what ways did your material decisions and means of construction influence your design?

In developing economies as such Peru's, we have to think carefully about the resources and materials with which we build. The condition of perpetual crisis and instability trained us to work with what's available, as people often do here. That doesn't condemn us to scarcity of means; it's mainly a matter of turning the gaze to the possibilities given to us by our culture, our climate and our landscape. We have access to some wonderful materials due to our country's extraordinary conditions. Materials for us are not only sand, cement and aggregates, all easily available in our coastal desert, but also culture, which comes from 5,000 years of civilization in the central Andes; our unique climate; place, that for us is always key to understand what we should do; program, which we like to see as a set of potential usages and not simply as a list of surfaces and relations between them; and technology, taking advantage of pre-industrial craftmanship and building processes. We work carefully, mixing these "materials" to give meaning to the essential elements of architecture: space, light, matter and time.

What do you want people to experience/take away from your work?

We want them to experience the same things we experienced when we saw great buildings: we want them to feel well in a place. We want them to feel as if they belong; more than understanding structure or showing historical types, or being modern, or whatever. It's experiential: feeling the shadows, the breezes, etc. A lot of what Grafton was saying during the biennale. Creating microcosms, a free space.

Tell us about phenomenology and your work. There are memories and traces of many modern precedents in the building. Are there influences that were particularly meaningful to you?

We don't want to be "phenomenological architects," but there are these things that always intervene in architecture. We studied at a time in Peru when there was no internet, and not even enough books. When we went to Europe, we realized how ignorant of architecture we were. But Europe was fixed and academic. So, we visited places and drew all the time. We have an obsession with visiting and experiencing architecture; and that's our phenomenology. Of course, we admired Mies, Wright, Kahn, and Le Corbusier—not for the theory, but for the experience of the buildings. We never start by searching for references or histories; the program and the site drive us. We don't look for the references, they appear. We love to discover who's influencing us—not before, but during. We don't research references until the idea of the project is firmly established.

MCHAP grew out of the modernist legacy that Mies helped to build. Where does this building sit on that spectrum?

Any disenchantment in Europe and North America with modern architecture's transformative power is not found in Latin America. Modern architecture came first to our countries as an image (not as a consequence) of future social change, and new technologies would be the vector of this change. Today, architects in Latin America are conscious that the future of the modern legacy is rooted in our own past, finding what is appropriate for our countries, what is available and meaningful for going forward and improving people's quality of life. By doing this, our work is based on a continuation of the modernist legacy, the belief in positive change that Mies fostered in each of his projects.

Catalogue of Works

0 50

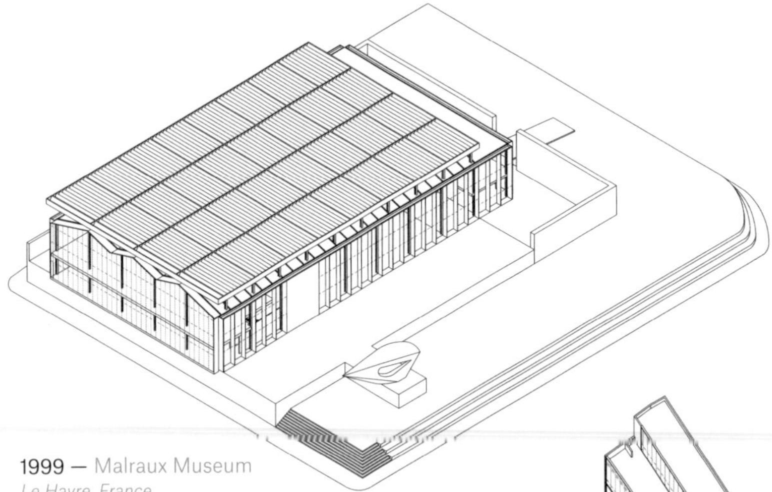

1999 — Malraux Museum
Le Havre, France
49°29'5.98"N | 0° 6'9.60"E

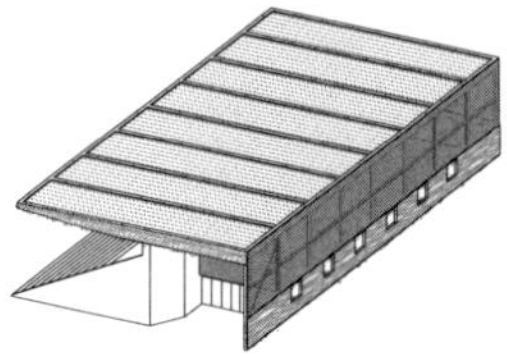

2005 — Rambouillet Racecourse
Rambouillet, France
48°38'10.95"N | 1°51'1.95"E

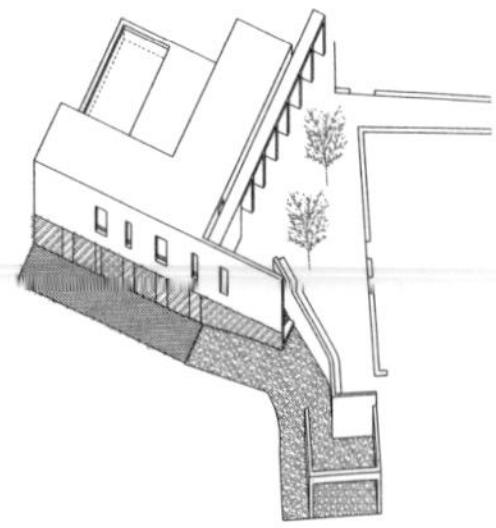

2005 — H House
Gers, France
43°33'26.06"N | 1° 1'33.97"E

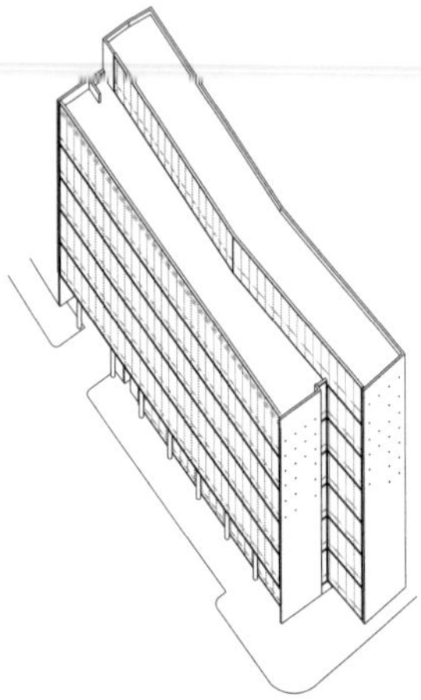

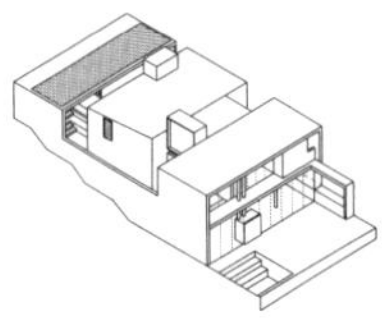

2001 — M House
Cañete, Peru
12°53'47.14"S | 76°30'34.18"O

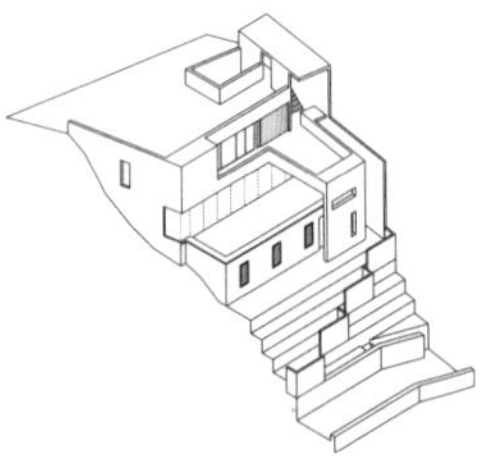

1998 — B House
Cañete, Peru
12°53'49.78"S | 76°30'35.11"O

2003 — Gambetta Building
Malakoff, Paris, France
48°49'25.05"N | 2°18'25.07"E

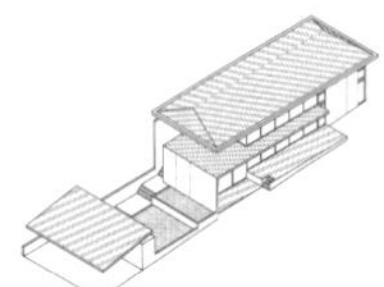

2006 — B&F House
Haute Savoie, France
46°18'45.68"N | 6°20'19.28"E

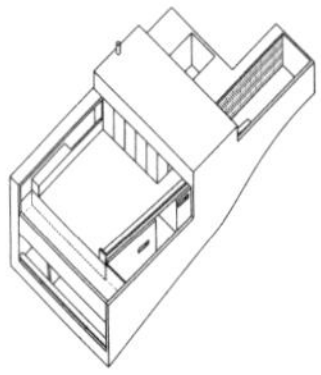

2003 — Equis House
Cañete, Peru
12°53'46.55"S | 76°30'34.50"O

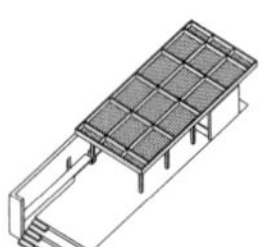

2006 — LE Kiosk
La Escondida, Peru
12°53'48.94"S | 76°30'30.35"O

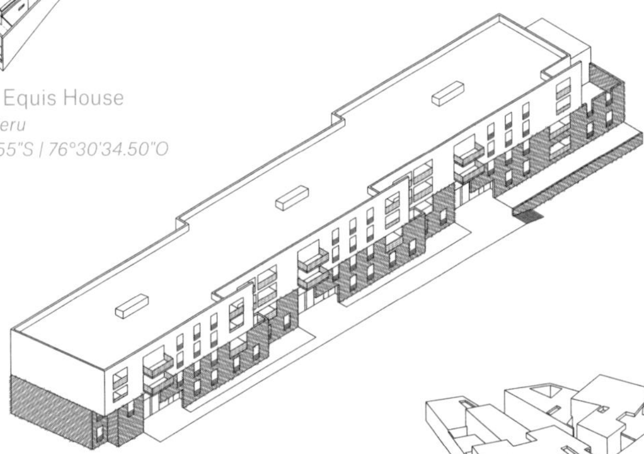

2005 — Victor Hugo Social Housing
Montreuil, Paris, France
48°51'42.16"N | 2°26'18.84"E

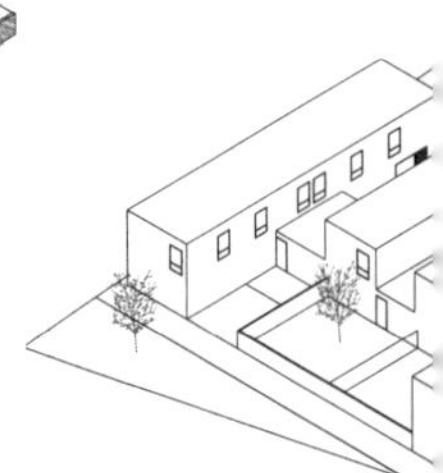

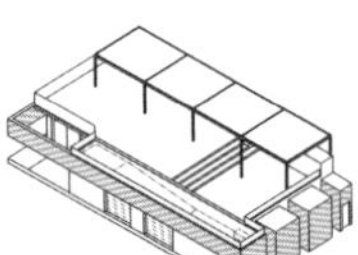

2009 — M4 House
Asia, Peru
12°46'39.41"S | 76°36'19.39"O

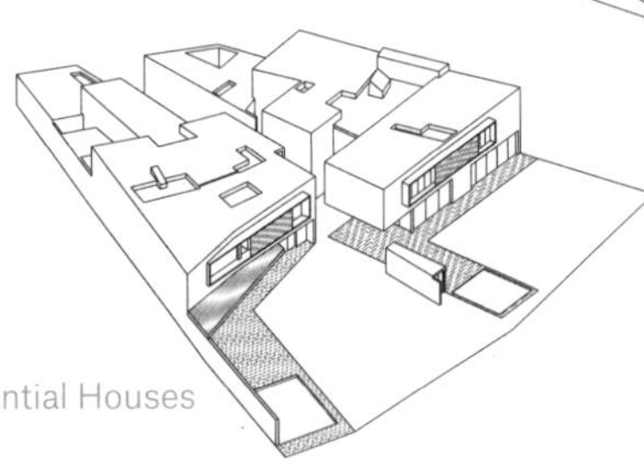

2009 — El Manantial Houses
Lima, Peru
12° 4'33.32"S | 76°54'17.66"O

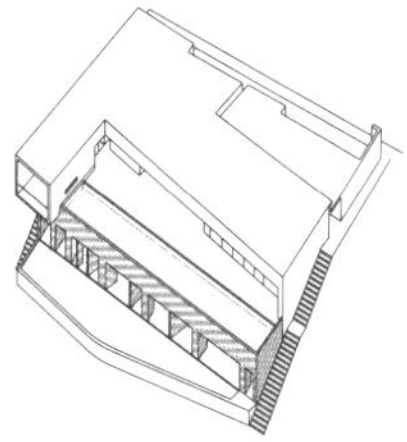

2007 — O2 House
Pucusana, Peru
12°26'34.52"S | 76°46'44.48"O

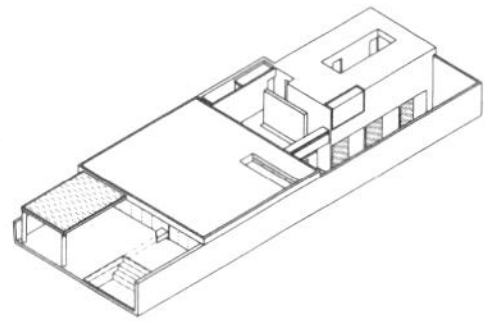

2007 — O House
Asia, Peru
12°45'55.66"S | 76°36'46.13"O

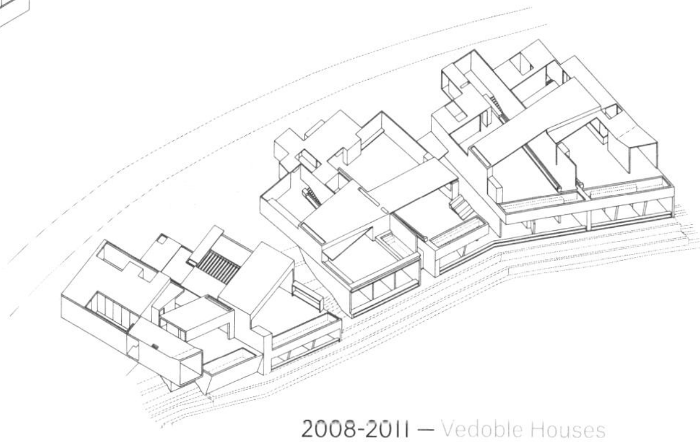

2008-2011 — Vedoble Houses
La Escondida, Peru
12°53'51.19"S | 76°30'33.68"O

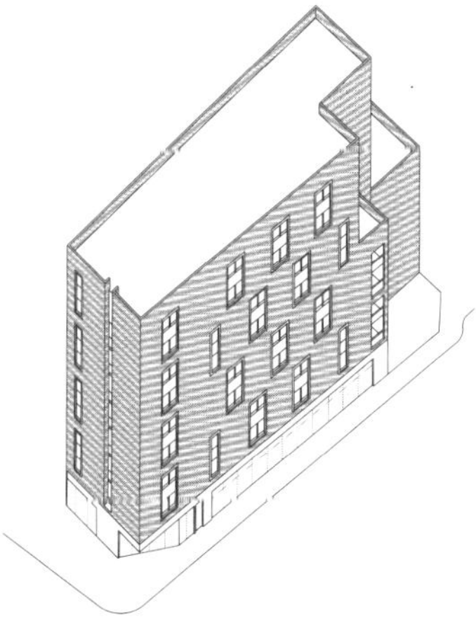

2009 — Frida Kahlo Residence
Montreuil, France
48°51'44.20"N | 2°26'35.65"E

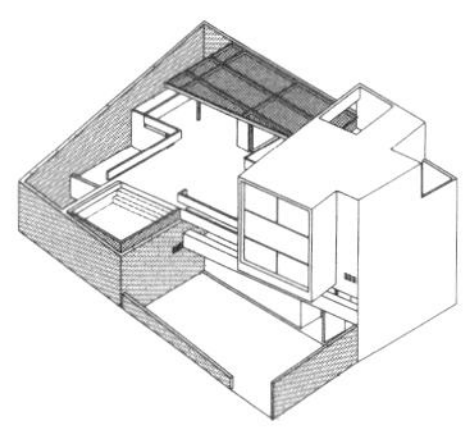

2008 — M3 House
Asia, Peru
12°45'2.48"S | 76°37'14.08"O

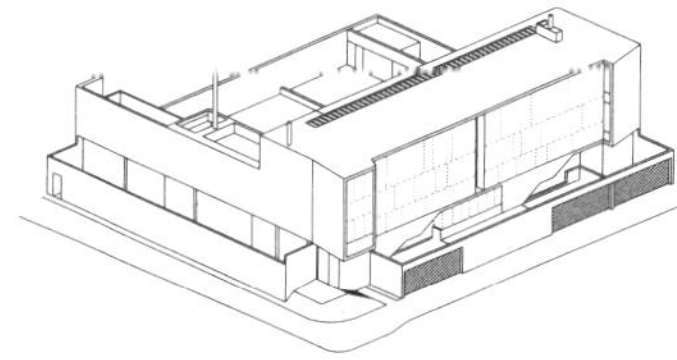

2010 — 3G Houses
Lima, Peru
12° 5'52.67"S | 77° 2'47.64"O

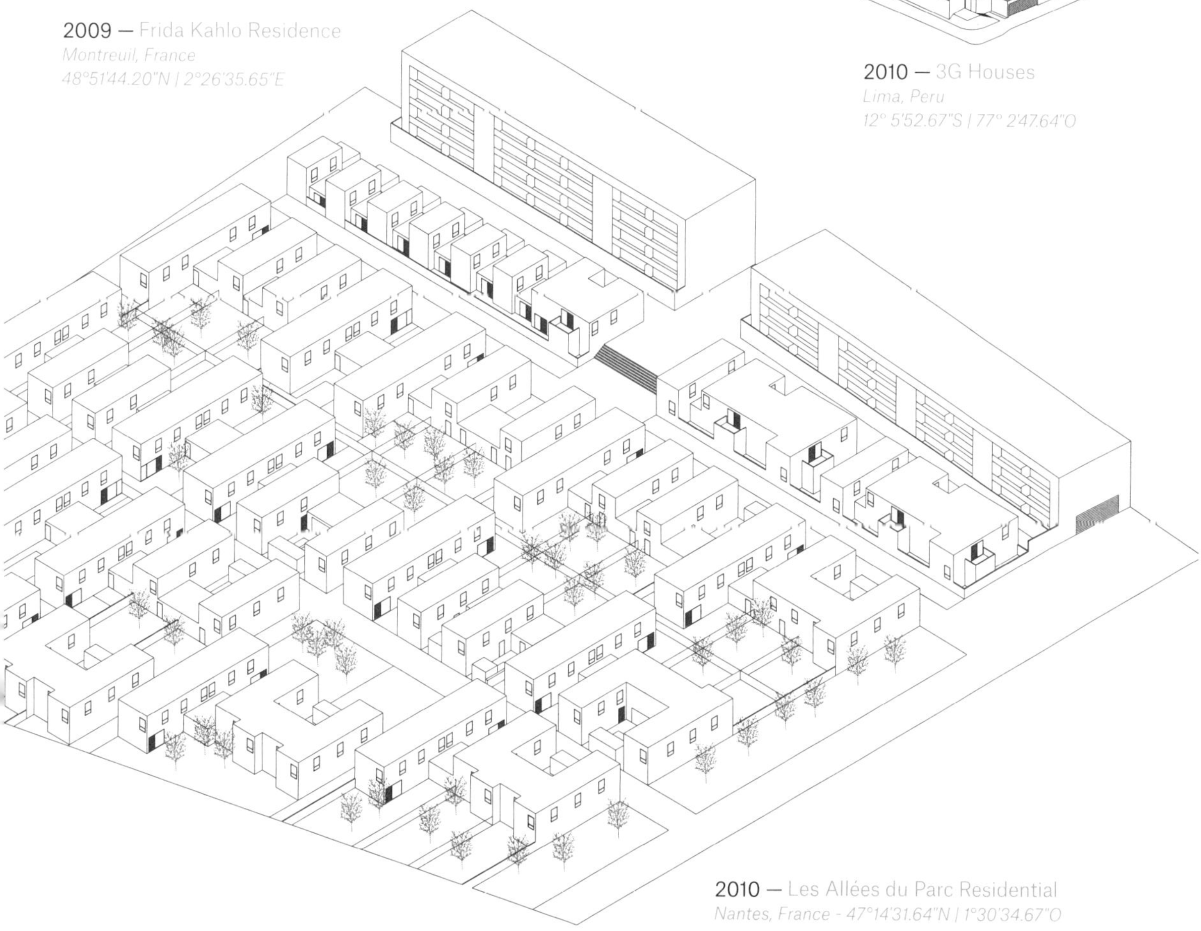

2010 — Les Allées du Parc Residential
Nantes, France - 47°14'31.64"N | 1°30'34.67"O

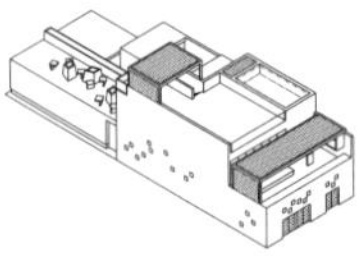

2010 — ZR House
Asia, Peru
12°46'9.36"S | 76°36'24.95"O

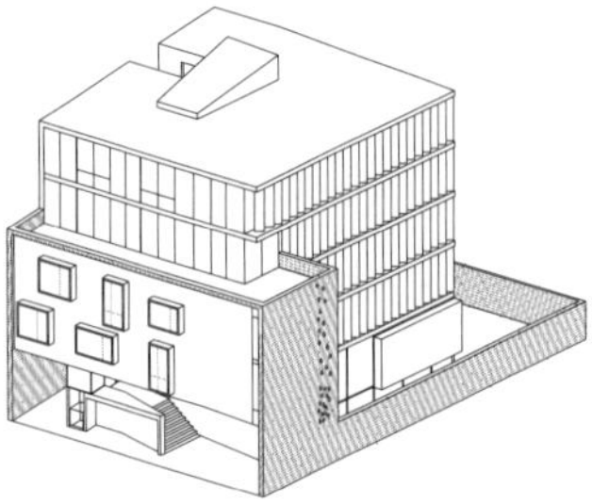

2010 — AS Building
Lima, Peru
12° 6'23.73"S | 77° 2'28.61"O

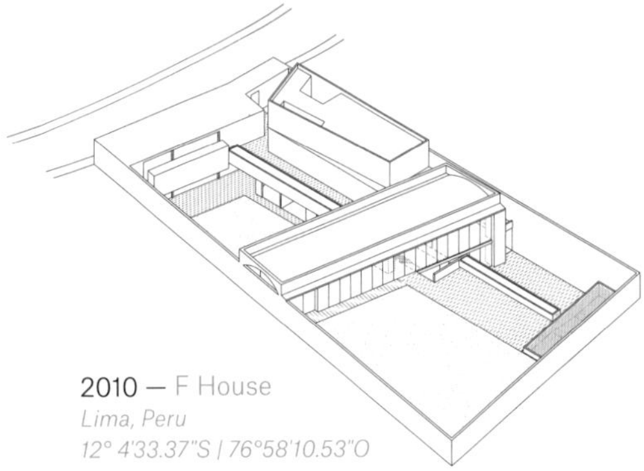

2010 — F House
Lima, Peru
12° 4'33.37"S | 76°58'10.53"O

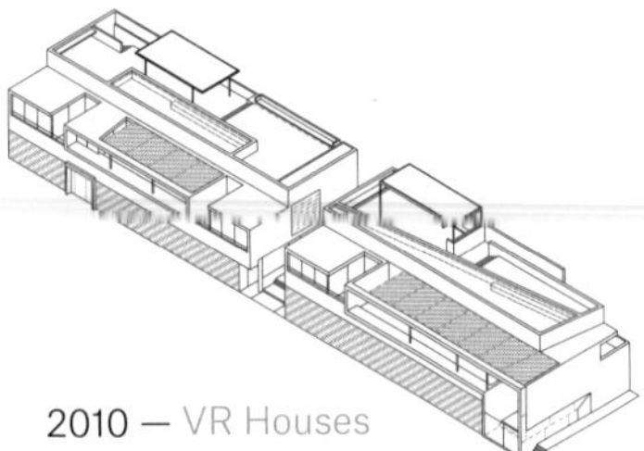

2010 — VR Houses
Cerro Colorado, Peru
13° 0'0.55"S | 76°29'27.34"O

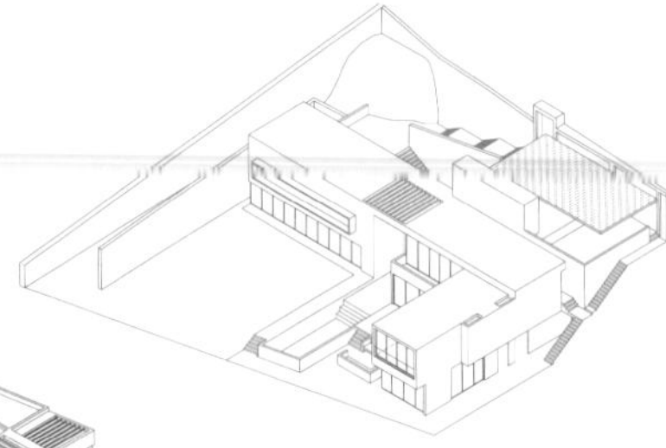

2010 — B3 House
Lima, Peru
12° 7'23.20"S | 76°58'22.05"O

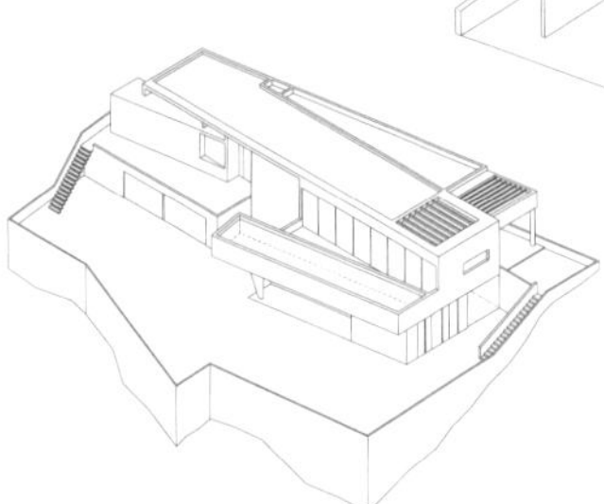

2010 — B2 House
Lima, Peru
12° 7'22.29"S | 76°58'21.41"O

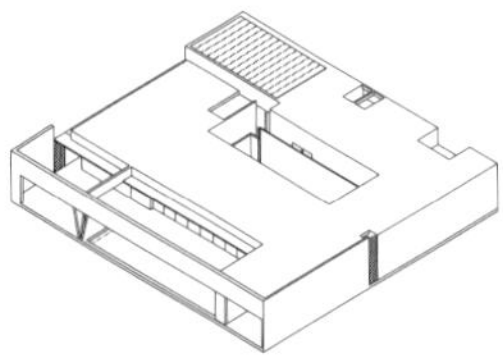

2011 — O3 House
Cerro Colorado, Peru
13° 0'0.20"S | 76°29'28.85"O

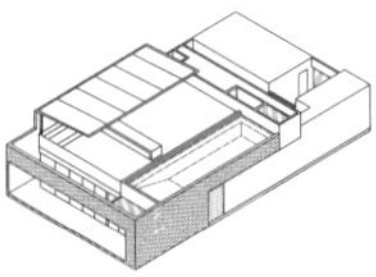

2011 — C2 House
Cerro Colorado, Peru
12°59'59.72"S | 76°29'29.47"O

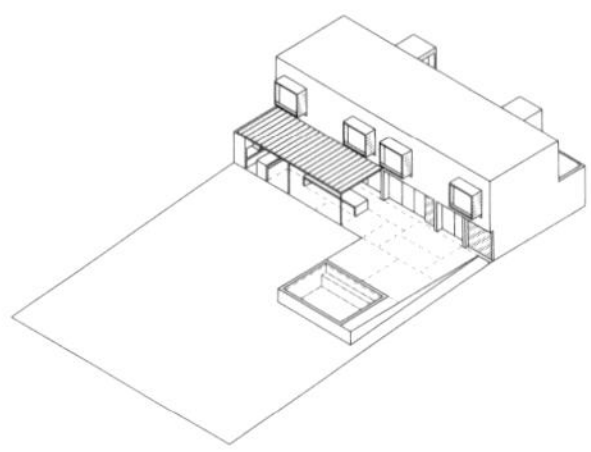

2011 — CR House
Chaclacayo, Peru
11°57'24.25"S | 76°43'41.17"O

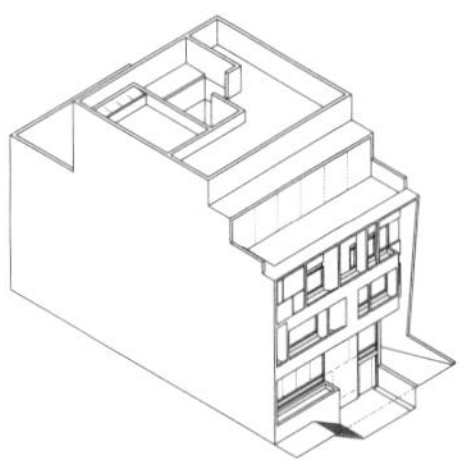

2012 — Townhouse El Olivar
Lima, Peru
12° 6'10.42"S | 77° 2'9.77"O

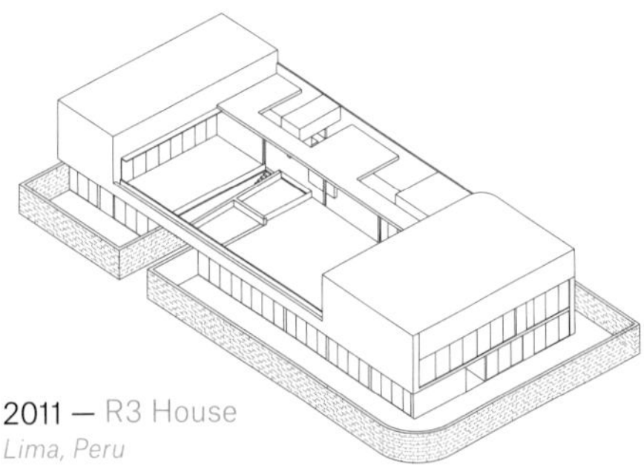

2011 — R3 House
Lima, Peru
12° 4'50.29"S | 76°58'21.29"O

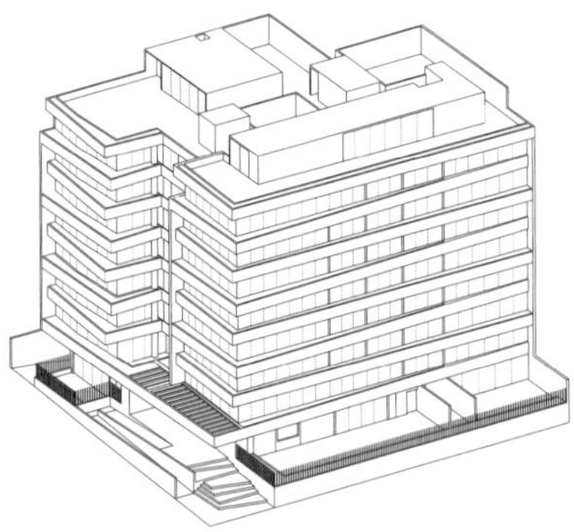

2012 — Chamberi Building
Lima, Peru
12° 6'48.70"S | 77° 2'25.06"O

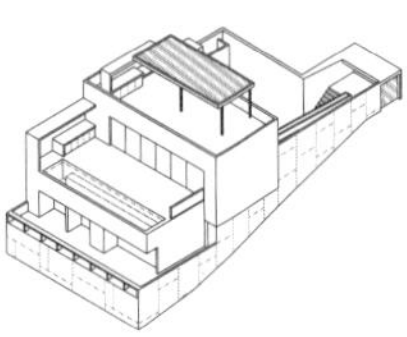

2011 — F3 House
La Escondida, Peru
12°53'53.76"S | 76°30'33.63"O

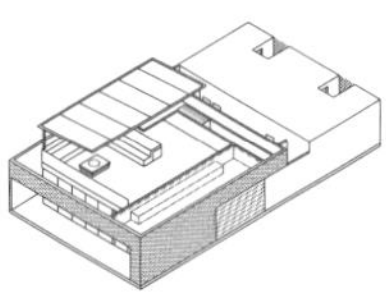

2011 — N House
Cerro Colorado, Peru
12°59'55.76"S | 76°29'30.74"O

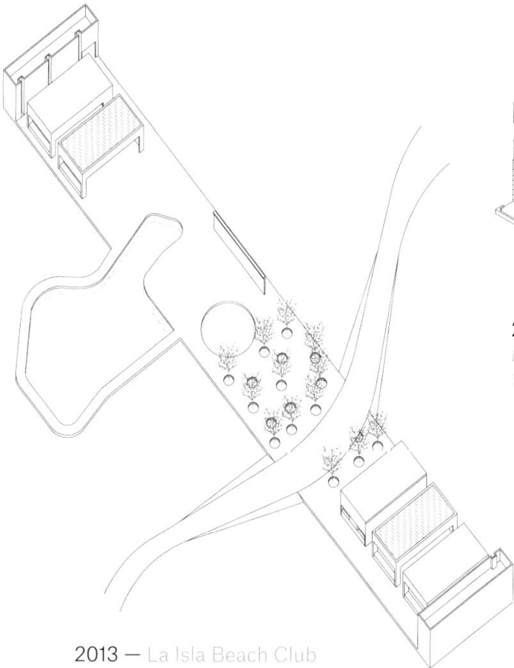

2013 — La Isla Beach Club
Asia, Peru
12°45'56.33"S | 76°36'33.37"O

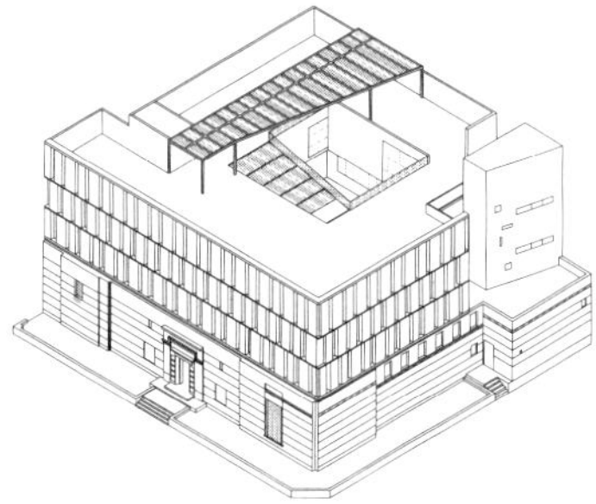

2012 — Visual Arts School
Lima, Peru
12° 7'21.12"S | 77° 2'23.20"O

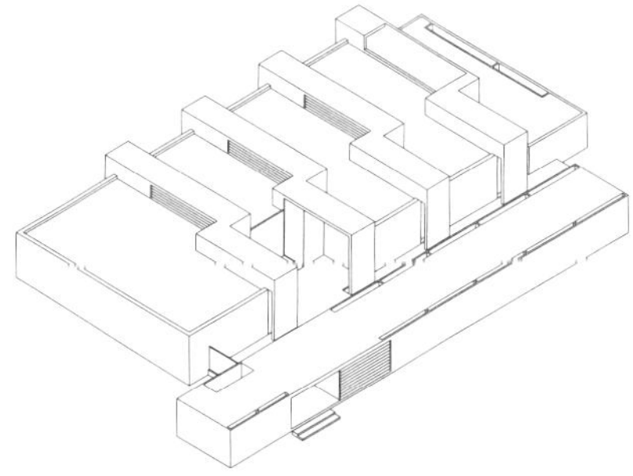

2012 — Paracas Museum
Opening year: 2016
Paracas, Peru
13°52'6.25"S | 76°16'22.64"O

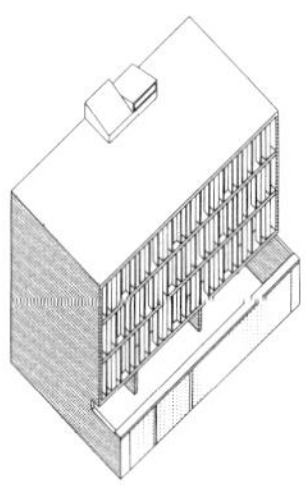

2013 — Dentaid Laboratories
Lima, Peru
12° 3'35.02"S | 76°57'27.17"O

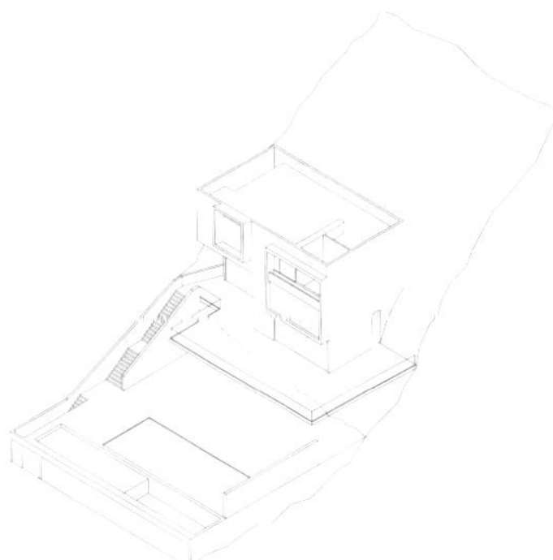

2012 — C House
Pucusana, Peru
12°28'8.47"S | 76°47'22.01"O

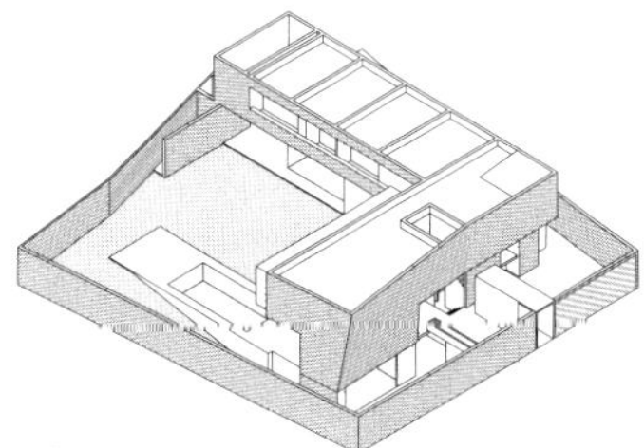

2013 — D House
Lima, Peru
12° 4'39.42"S | 76°56'22.00"O

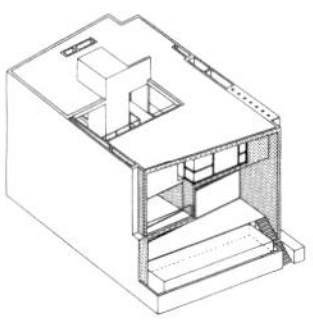

2013 — M6 House
Punta Hermosa, Peru
12°20'19.60"S | 76°49'11.37"O

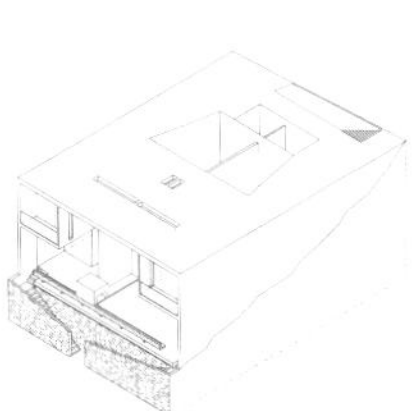

2013 — L Houses
Pucusana, Peru
12°26'40.08"S | 76°46'57.80"O

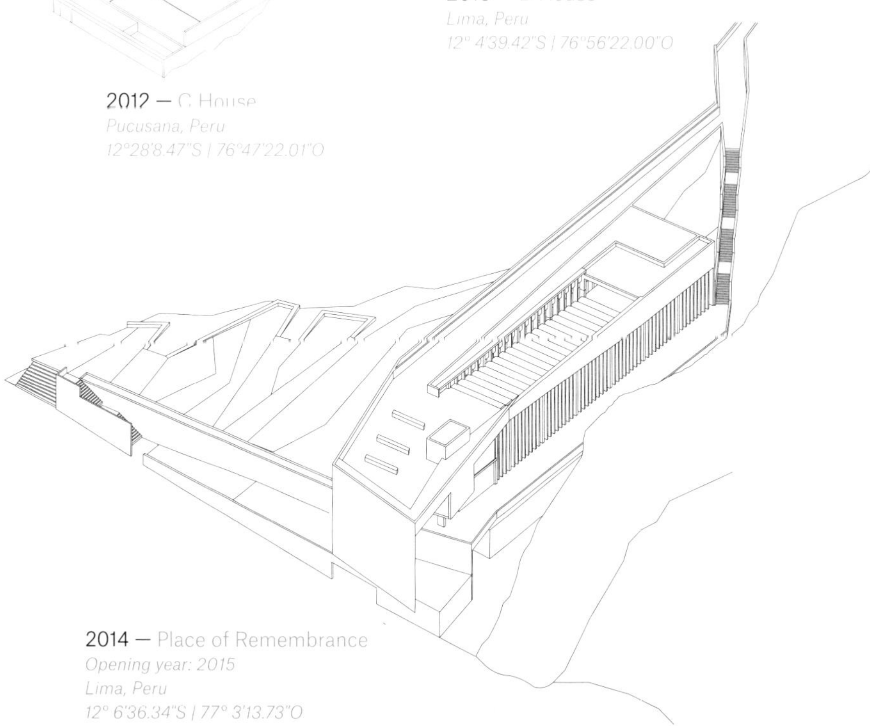

2014 — Place of Remembrance
Opening year: 2015
Lima, Peru
12° 6'36.34"S | 77° 3'13.73"O

0 50

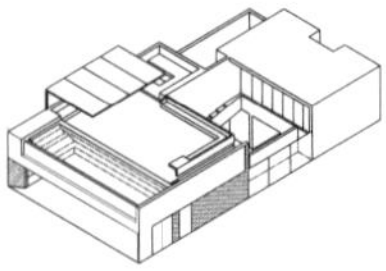

2014 — R5 House
Cerro Colorado, Peru
13° 0'2.42"S | 76°29'26.95"O

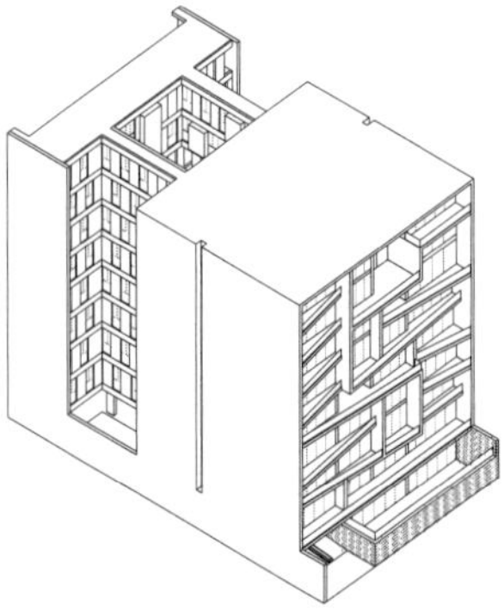

2014 — Las Dalias Building
Lima, Peru
12° 7'54.89"S | 77° 1'44.23"O

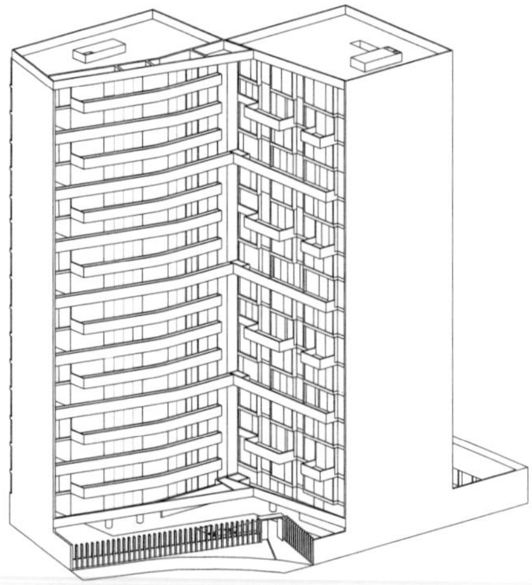

2014 — MC Building
Lima, Peru
12° 7'17.76"S | 77° 2'29.29"O

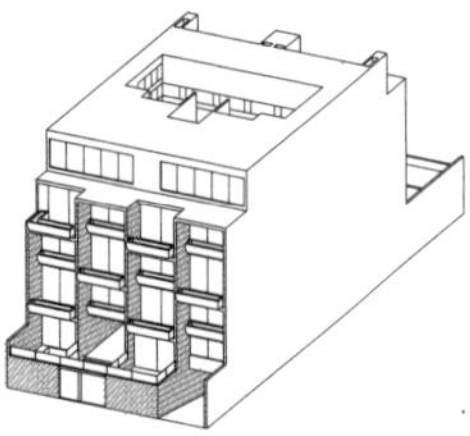

2014 — Venecia Building
Lima, Peru
12° 6'33.08"S | 76°59'30.89"O

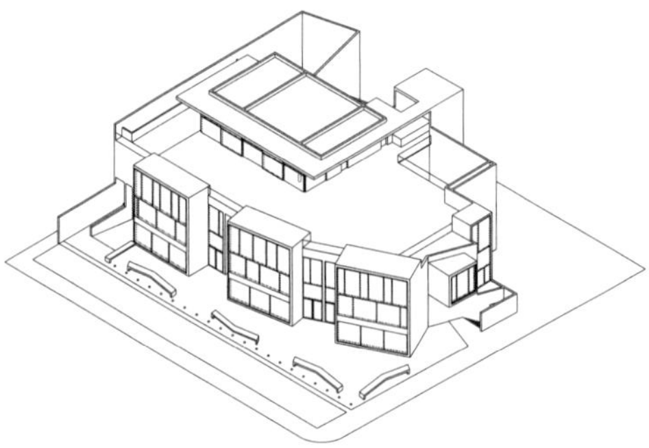

2014 — El Bosque Boutiques
Lima, Peru
12° 5'43.44"S | 77° 2'0.82"O

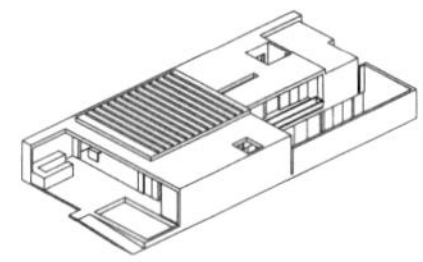

2015 — B3 House
Asia, Peru
12°46'29.28"S | 76°36'31.70"O

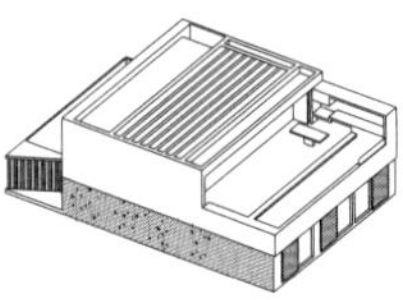

2015 — D2 House
Asia, Peru
12°46'27.90"S | 76°36'29.13"O

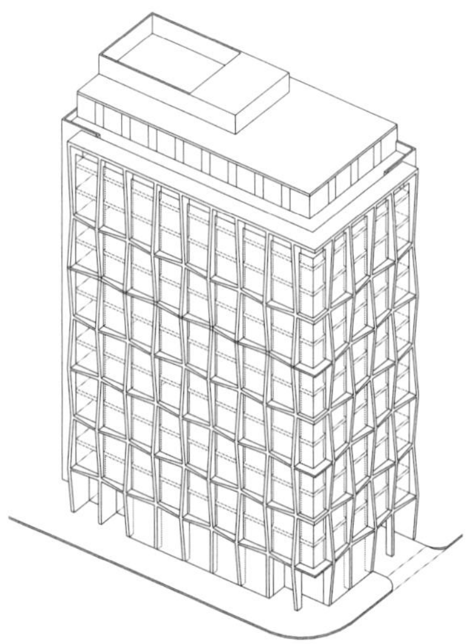

2015 — Beehive 1 and 2 Offices
Lima, Peru
12° 5'0.98"S | 77° 2'9.45"O

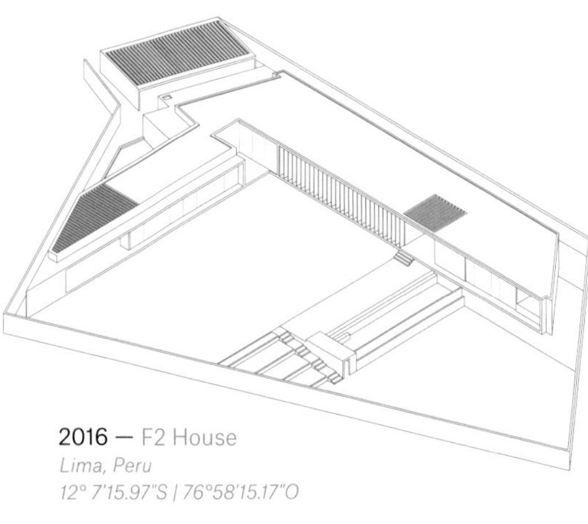

2016 — F2 House
Lima, Peru
12° 7'15.97"S | 76°58'15.17"O

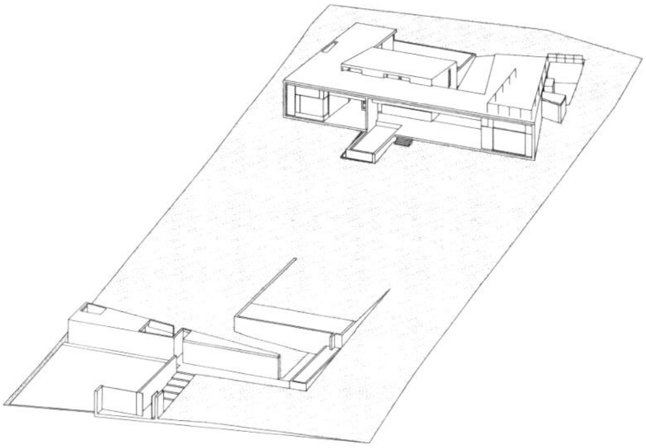

2015 — T House
Pachacamac, Peru
12°14'46.52"S | 76°50'48.71"O

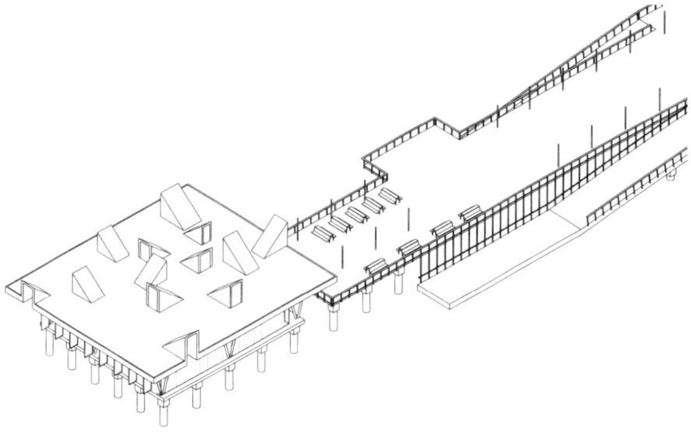

2016 — AMARdeLIMA Restaurant
Lima, Peru
12° 9'51.32"S | 77° 1'56.45"O

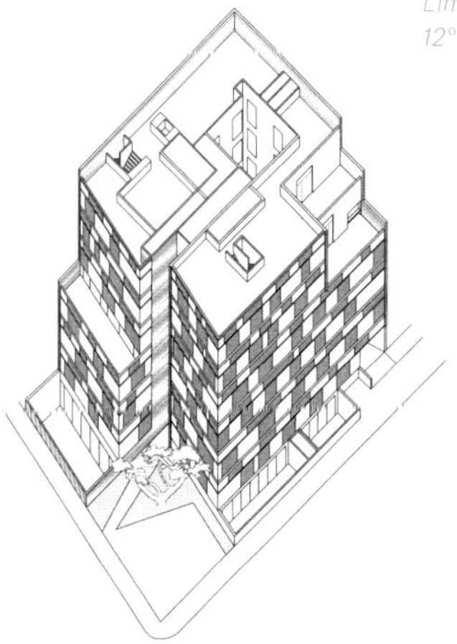

2015 — La Ponciana Building
Lima, Peru
12° 5'53.95"S | 77° 2'7.16"O

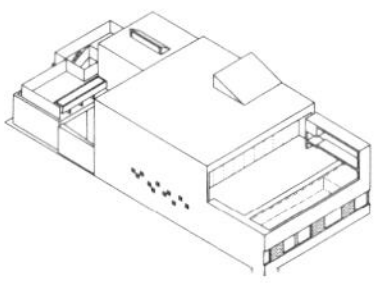

2016 — L2 House
Asia, Peru
12°46'9.24"S | 76°36'35.27"O

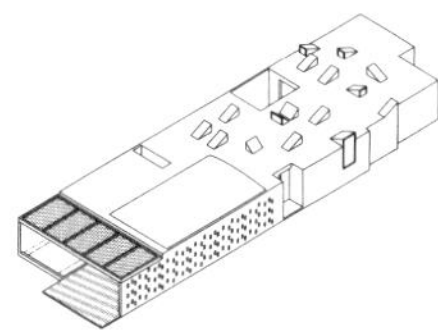

2016 — D4 House
Asia, Peru
12°46'17.57"S | 76°36'36.06"O

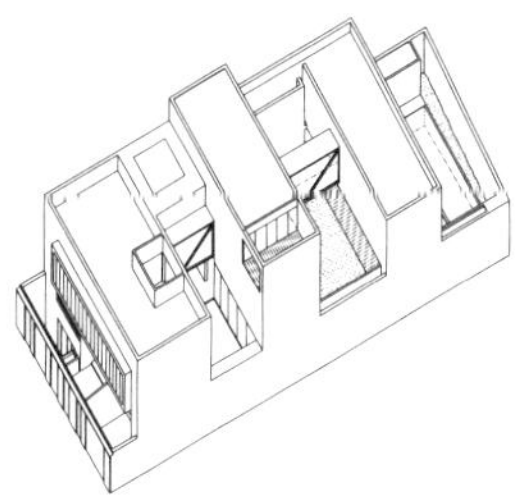

2016 — A4 House
Lima, Peru
12° 6'20.56"S | 77° 3'12.88"O

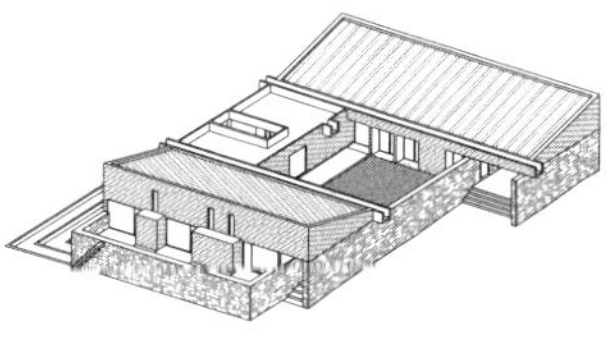

2016 — B5 House
Cusco, Peru
13°19'26.30"S | 72° 3'17.12"O

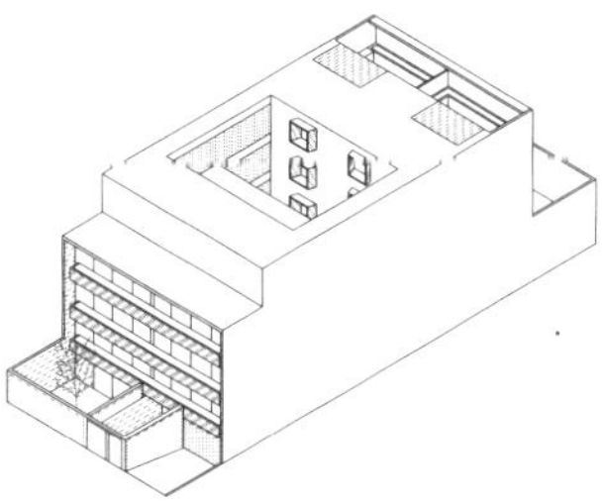

2017 — P Building
Lima, Peru
12° 6'16.94"S | 76°58'52.50"O

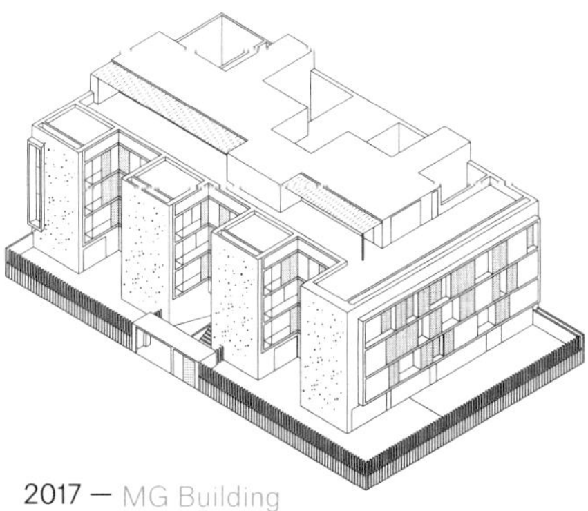

2017 — MG Building
Lima, Peru
12° 7'6.48"S | 76°58'53.68"O

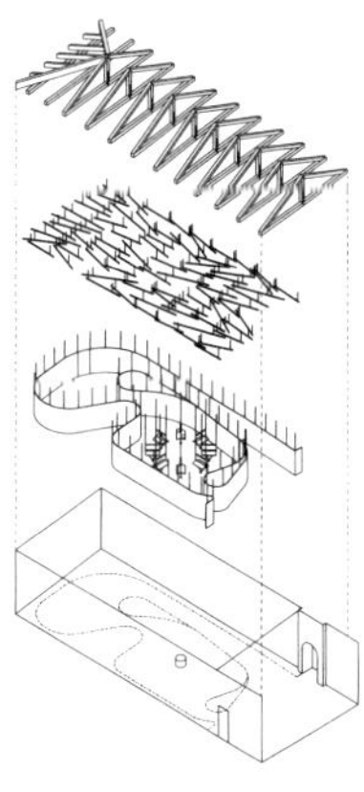

2016 — Peruvian Pavilion, Biennale of Venice
Venice, Italy
45°26'2.09"N | 12°21'18.59"E

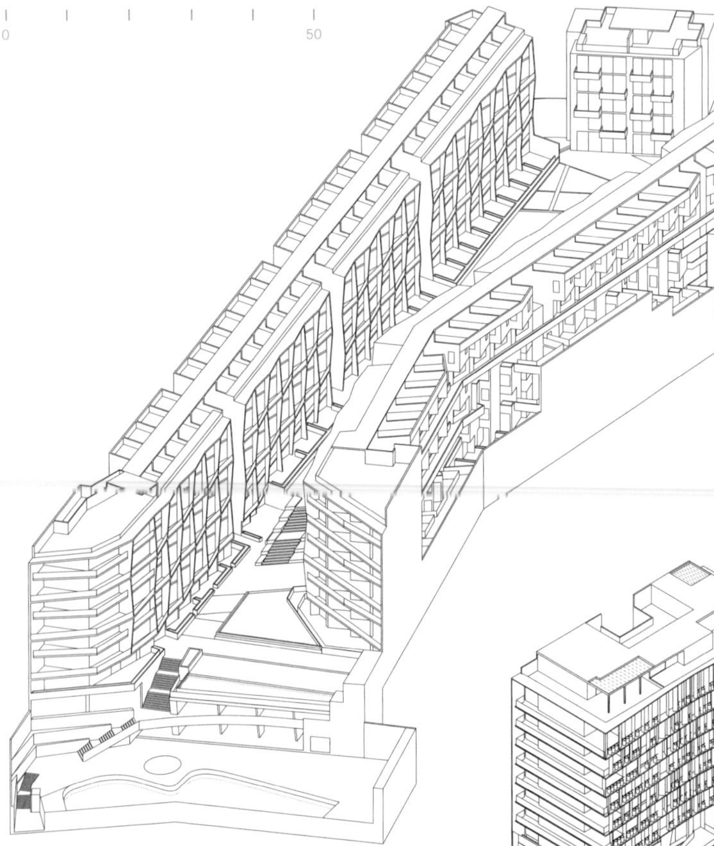

2017- 2020 — Ocean Reef Housing Complex
San Bartolo, Peru
12°23'0.30"S | 76°47'4.65"O

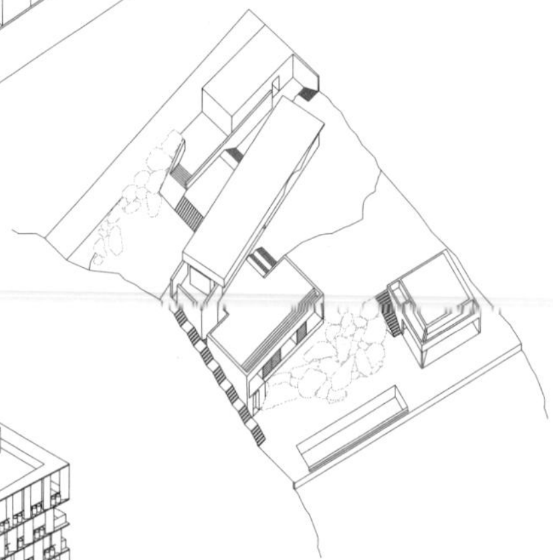

2017 — C3 House
Ancón, Peru
11°46'5.44"S | 77°11'38.50"O

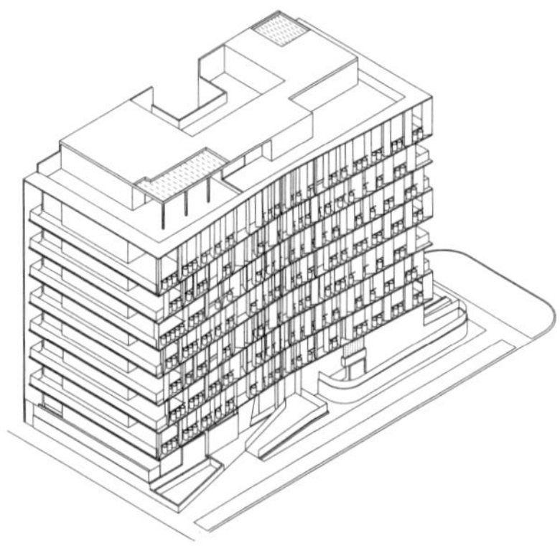

2017 — NU Building
Lima, Peru
12° 6'38.86"S | 77° 2'35.20"O

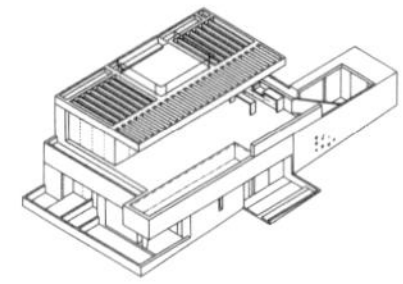

2018 — M7 House
La Escondida, Peru
12°53'47.72"S | 76°30'32.40"O

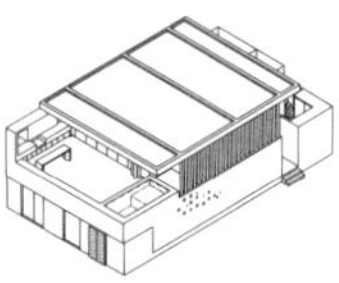

2018 — VO House
Asia, Peru
12°46'18.41"S | 76°36'25.32"O

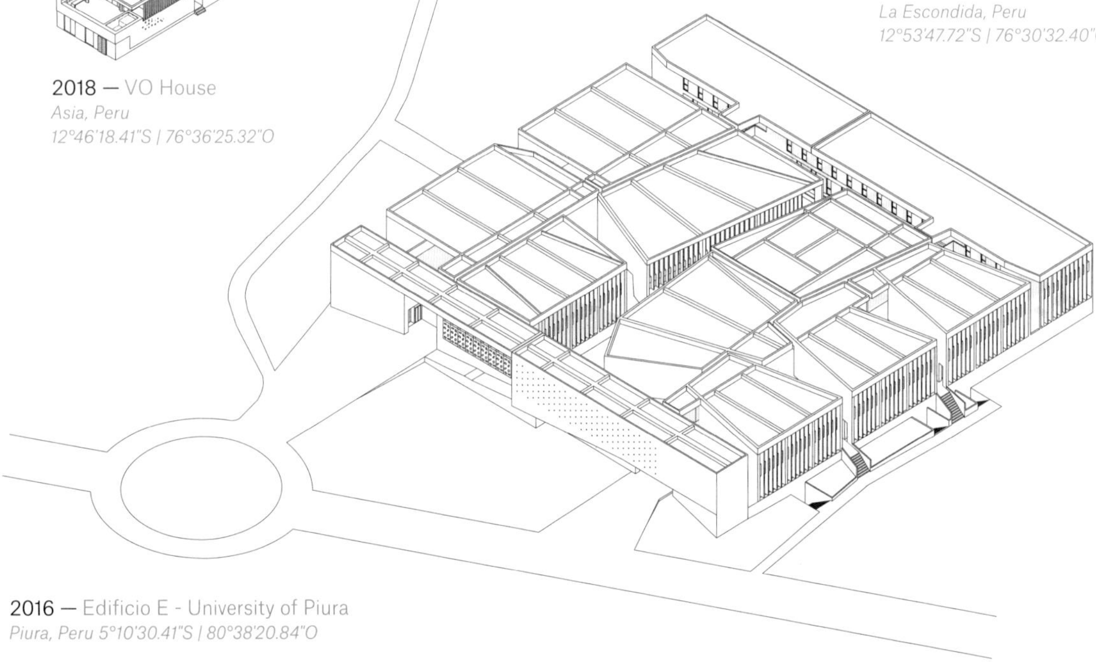

2016 — Edificio E - University of Piura
Piura, Peru 5°10'30.41"S | 80°38'20.84"O

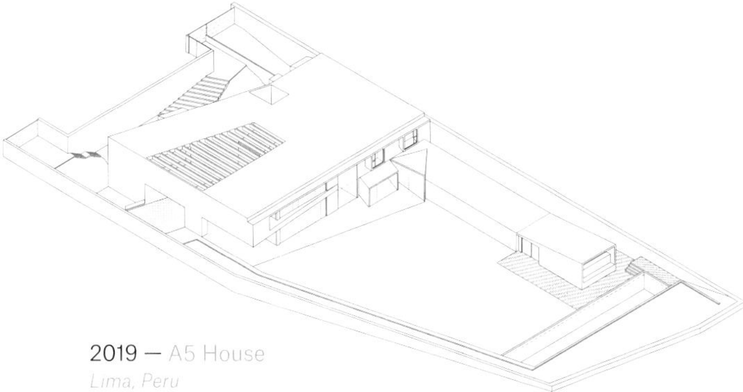

2019 — A5 House
Lima, Peru
12° 7'8.93"S | 76°58'11.35"O

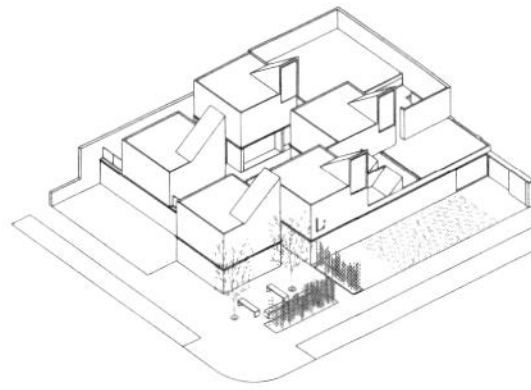

2019 — Limaná Restaurant
Lima, Peru
12° 6'17.81"S | 77° 3'24.09"O

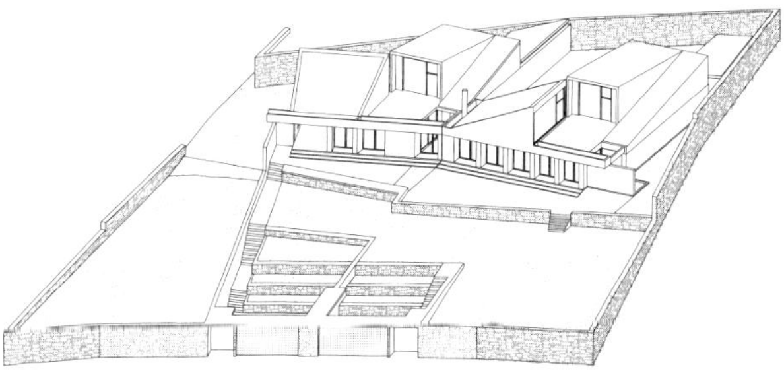

2018 — Huayoccari Houses
Cusco, Peru
13°19'29.75"S | 72° 3'7.56"O

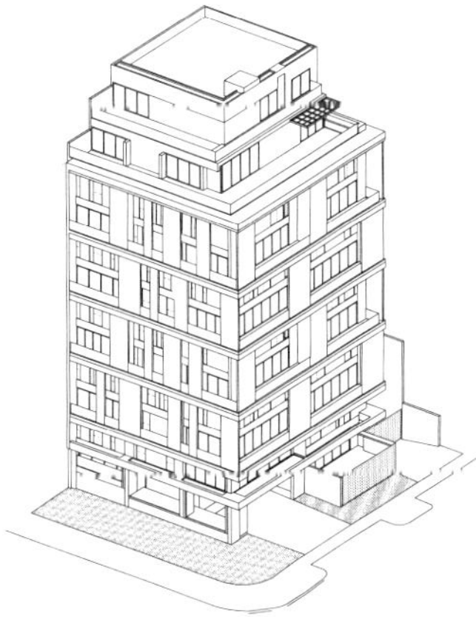

2019 — Lithos Building
Lima, Peru
12° 5'44.14"S | 77° 2'37.46"O

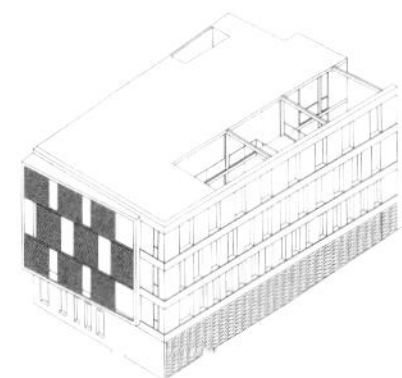

2020 — Colina Building
Lima, Peru
12° 8'46.83"S | 77° 1'25.26"O

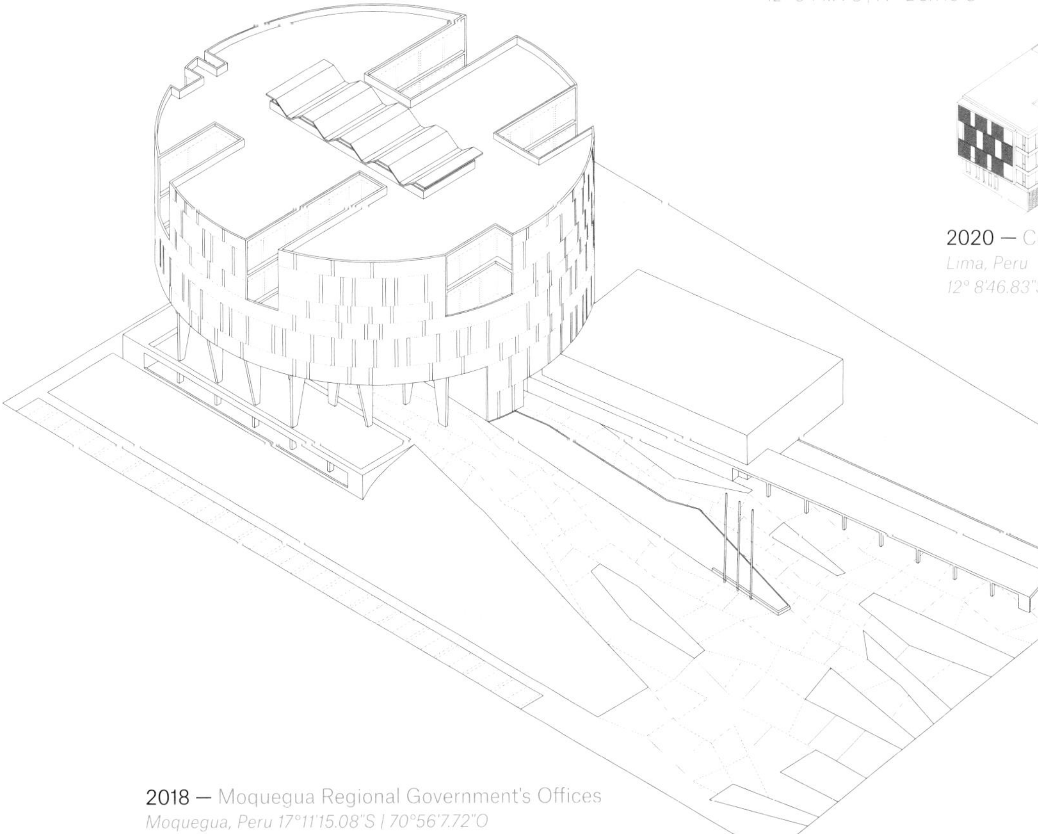

2018 — Moquegua Regional Government's Offices
Moquegua, Peru 17°11'15.08"S | 70°56'7.72"O

Sandra Barclay (Lima, 1967) studied architecture at the Ricardo Palma University (Lima, 1990) and subsequently at the Paris-Belleville Architecture School (France, 1994), where she was awarded the Robert Camelot Prize for best thesis project in France. She co-founded Barclay & Crousse Architecture the same year. In 2000 she held Fulbright and American Institute of Architects scholarships. In 2013 she graduated with a Masters in Landscape and Territory from Diego Portales University in Chile. Since 2006 she has been associate professor at the Pontifical Catholic University of Peru, and visiting professor at the National University of Litoral (Argentina, 2012), Yale University (2019) and the University of Virginia (2020). In 2018 she received the Women in Architecture award from London's *Architect's Journal* and the *Architectural Review*. In 2018 she participated together with Jean Pierre in the main exhibition of the Venice Biennale of Architecture. In 2019 she was named an honorary member of the American Institute of Architects and of France's Academy of Architecture.

Jean Pierre Crousse (Lima, 1963) studied architecture at the Ricardo Palma University (Lima, 1987) and subsequently at the Milan Polytechnic (Italy, 1989). He obtained a Masters in Landscape and Territory at the Diego Portales University in 2013. After working at Henri Ciriani's architecture office for five years, he co-founded Barclay & Crousse Architecture in Paris in 2004. He began his teaching career at the Paris-Belleville School of Architecture (1999-2005). He has been associate professor at the Pontifical Catholic University of Peru since 2006, and director of the Masters in Architecture and Project Processes since 2017. He has been visiting professor at the universities of Los Andes (Colombia, 2011-2012), Litoral (Argentina, 2012), Harvard Graduate School of Design (2015), Yale (2019), and Virginia (2020), the last three in the United States. He was awarded the Special Mention of the Jury for co-curating, together with Sandra Barclay, Peru's pavilion at the 15th Venice Biennale of Architecture. He has served as an international jury member for the Mies Crown Hall Americas Prize (2016) and for the 11th Iberoamerican Biennial (2019). He has been an honorary member of France's Academy of Architecture since 2019.

Miquel Adrià (Barcelona, 1956) is an architect from the School of Architecture of Barcelona / UPC and PhD Universidad Europea de Madrid. In 1994 he moved to Mexico, and since then combines practice, teaching and criticism. He has published more than thirty books on Mexican and Latin American architecture. He is the director of Arquine and the Festival of Architecture and City MEXTRÓPOLI. He is director of the School of Architecture at CENTRO.

Mario Vargas Llosa (Arequipa, 1936). Although he had already written a play in Piura and published a book of short stories, *Los jefes*, which received the Leopoldo Alas Prize, his literary career took off with the publication of *La ciudad y los perros*, which was awarded the Biblioteca Breve Prize (1962) and Premio de la Crítica (1963). In 1965 he published his second novel, *La Casa Verde*, which won the Premio de la Crítica and Rómulo Gallegos International Prize. Later, he wrote plays (*La señorita de Tacna*, *Kathie y el hipopótamo*, *La Chunga*, *El loco de los balcones*, *Ojos bonitos, cuadros feos*, *Las mil noches y una noche*), studies and essays (*La orgía perpetua*, *La verdad de las mentiras*, *La tentación de lo imposible*, *El viaje a la ficción*, *La civilización del espectáculo*, *La llamada de la tribu*), a memoir (*El pez en el agua*), short stories (*Los cachorros*) and novels: *Conversación en La Catedral*, *Pantaleón y las visitadoras*, *La tía Julia y el escribidor*, *La guerra del fin del mundo*, *Historia de Mayta*, *¿Quién mató a Palomino Molero?*, *El hablador*, *Elogio de la madrastra*, *Lituma en los Andes*, *Los cuadernos de don Rigoberto*, *La fiesta del Chivo*, *El Paraíso en la otra esquina*, *Travesuras de la niña mala*, *El sueño del celta*, *El héroe discreto*, *Cinco Esquinas*, and *Tiempos recios*. He has received the most important literary awards, in addition to those already mentioned, including the Cervantes Prize, the Prince of Asturias Award, the PEN/Nabokov Award, the Grinzane Cavour, and the Nobel Prize in Literature 2010. His work has been translated into more than forty languages. Since 1994 he has been a member of the Royal Spanish Academy.

Dirk Denison, Professor of Architecture at Illinois Institute of Technology, is an award-winning architect, longtime educator, and dedicated supporter of the arts. His nationally recognized firm, Dirk Denison Architects, has developed its own modernist vocabulary in multiple scales of built works from New York to California, with a particular expertise in housing, community-based design, and campus planning. As Director of the Mies Crown Hall Americas Prize, he has convened and moderated events, workshops, and publications that feature a global network of collaborating practitioners, clients, writers and theorists, and civic leaders from throughout the Americas. His first monograph, *Dirk Denison 10 Houses*, was published by Actar in December 2018.

Reed Kroloff is dean of the College of Architecture at Illinois Institute of Technology. He also has served as director of the Cranbrook Academy of Art, dean of the Tulane University School of Architecture, and editor-in-chief of *Architecture* magazine. Kroloff is a Rome Prize recipient, has exhibited at the Venice Biennale, and has been published widely. His private practice has managed architect selections for universities, museums, governments, non-profits, and the private sector.

Acknowledgments

We would like to express our thanks to the Mies Crown Hall Americas Prize and the Illinois Institute of Technology for making this book a reality and for motivating us to explore our own work. To Miquel Adrià, Andrea Griborio, and Brenda Soto at Arquine for their tireless efforts in editing and publishing this project. Special thanks to Mario Vargas Llosa for his deep conviction in the need to make the Place of Remembrance a reality, and for the text he so generously wrote for this book. We are grateful to Reed Kroloff, Dean of IIT, Dirk Denison, Director of the MCHAP, Miquel Adrià, Director of Arquine, for the texts and the interview that enrich this book. To Cristóbal Palma, whose gaze and images help provide a consistent and coherent understanding of our projects with consistency and coherence.

We thank our partners with whom we have shared project adventures at the Atelier Nord Sud with Jean Marc Viste and Guilhem Roustan and on specific projects with Emmanuelle and Laurent Beaudouin (Museo Malraux, Montreuil Victor Hugo), Paolo Tarabusi (Centro Empresarial Gambetta), Oscar Gonzales-Moix (Las Dalias Building), UA Studio - NUBT (Beehive 1 and 2 Business Center, Flat Arequipa).

We thank our clients, who with the trust placed in us have made these projects a reality. In France: Ville du Havre, Société du Cheval Français, Marignan Bouwfonds, Sopic - Ville de Montreuil, Bleecker Group, Group Expansiel Promotion, Claudie et Patrick Hardy, Patrick Boidin. In Peru: Asociación Civil Playa La Escondida, Ciesa y Covilar, Azores Group, Club La Isla, Inversiones Alternas, AECID - Ministry of Culture, Dentaid, High Level Commission for the Construction of the Place of Remembrance - UNDP, Tucán Inversiones, Global Home, Flat Inmobiliaria, Yes Perú, Club Regatas Lima, Mota-Engil, Patronato Cultural del Perú, Pramin, Octagon, University of Piura, Quatro Inmobiliaria, Define Inmobiliaria, Urbi - Moquegua Regional Government, Edgard Barriga, Justo Monteghirfo, Rosario and Pedro Olguin, Elise and César Ortiz, Adriana Loli and Olav Maaland, Gaby and Alfredo Munda, Daniella Boero and Francisco Vásquez, Patricia Zolezzi and Luis Alfonso Carrera, Francisca and Teresa Graña, Daniela Rota and Mario Ricci, Alberto Guía, Valerie Crousse and Bernardo Sambra, Marisa Rastelli, Daniela Belmont and Rafel Franco, Monica Ripamonti and Pedro Zavala, Claudia Garrido and José Vila, Janette Londoño and Chale Ramírez, Milagros Christen and José Ostolaza, Carlos Cornejo, Pamela Molla and Renzo Brazzoduro, Maria Jesus de la Fuente and Marco Brazzoduro, Giuliana Rastelli, Alfredo Bryce, Larissa Belmont and Victor Riesser, Tati Fernandini and Carlos Navarro, Dora Cruz and Miguel Flores, Carmen and Steve Dixon, Marisa Gonzales and Rafael Calda, Estrella Musiris, Rafo and Edgardo Llosa, Fernando Rodriquez, Mónica Correa and Alfonso Bustamante, Ljuvica and Gustavo de las Casas, Gada and Diego Farah, Mariana and Edward Barclay, Cuchi Gonzales and Rafael Arbulú, Julie Lindley, Rocío Bustamante and Ricardo García Rosell, Yvonne and Hernán Tejada, Anita Belaunde, Jessica and Sandra Van Oordt, María Luisa and Julio Malo, Caroll and Ricardo Caillaux, Ana María León and David de la Torre, Paola and Manuel Abusada.

To all those who have worked with us in the studio over the years to create a unique culture, which is reflected in this book: Karla Pilco, Melissa Apolaya, Vhal Del Solar, Rodrigo Apolaya, Paulo Shimabukuro, Juan Miguel Chinchay, Arnaud Casmajor, Margarita Macera, Oscar Malaspina, Arnaud Casemajor, Carlos Fernández, Rosa Aguirre, Sebastián Cilloniz, Alessandra Calmell, Enrique Llatas, María Isabel Pineda, Martín Montañez, Pamela Acuña, Alejandro Zamudio, Fernando Quiñonez, Eduardo Zambrano, Belén Desmaison, Alfredo Castro, Martha Leiva, Ernesto Apolaya, Chelsea Lee, Silvia Pittman, Bleker Ruiz, Alejandro Muro, Andrea Otero, Diego Torres, Tommaso Cigarini, Esteban Martínez Bacigaluppi, David Leininger, Walmir Collazos, Betty Chávez, Elodie Fichard, Fernando Tuesta, Patricia Díaz, Edwin Lam, Stanislas Naudeau, Cloe Naughton, John Mauricio, Lucía Uribe, Carlos Teruya.

To our parents, for their unconditional encouragement throughout our lives, and to our children, Tilsa and Mateo, who have grown up alongside these projects and supported us with their patience and understanding.

Barclay & Crousse. Landscapes of Intimacy was printed and bound in November 2020. It was printed on 120gsm IKPP paper and set in typefaces of the Atlas Grotesk family. The print run was 2,000 copies.